T0083080

STRUM & SING
THE
6 CHORD
SONGBOOK

Cherry Lane Music Company
Director of Publications/Project Editor: Mark Phillips

ISBN: 978-1-60378-789-5

Visit our website at www.cherrylaneprint.com

Contents

Accidentally in Love
from the Motion Picture SHREK 2

Words and Music by
Adam F. Duritz, Dan Vickrey, David Immergluck, Matthew Malley and David Bryson

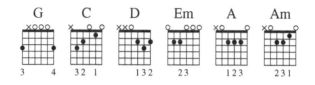

Intro

| G | | C | | G | | D | | |

| G | | C | | Em | | A | | C | | |

Verse 1

G |C |
So she said, "What's the problem, baby?"

G |C |Em
What's the problem? I don't know. Well, maybe I'm in love (love).

                    |A |C |
Think about it, every time I think about it, can't stop thinking 'bout it.

G |C |
How much longer will it take to cure this?

G |C |Em
Just to cure it 'cause I can't ignore it if it's love (love).

              |A
Makes me wanna turn around and face me

   |D |C ||
But I don't know nothing 'bout love. Ah.

Chorus 1

G   Am   C | D |
Come on, come on, turn   a little faster.

G   Am   C | D |
Come on, come on, the world   will follow after.

G   Am
Come on, come on,

C | D   Em |A |C | ||
'Cause everybody's after love.

Verse 2

```
     G               |C                  |
     So I said I'm a snowball running.
     G                       |C
     Running down into the spring that's coming.
        |Em              |A              |C
All this   love melting under blue skies, belting out sunlight,
           |G
Shimmering love.
           |C              |G                |
Well, baby, I surrender to the strawberry ice cream.
C                      |Em
Never ever end of all this   love.
        |A                        |D           |C            ||
Well, I didn't mean to do it, but there's no escaping your love.   Ah.
```

Bridge 1

```
Em              |C                |G
     These lines of lightning mean we're never alone,
Am   |        N.C.    ||
Never alone, no, no.
```

Chorus 2

```
G       Am      C    |      D      |
Come on, come on, move  a little closer.
G       Am      C    |          D      |
Come on, come on, I want  to hear you whisper.
G       Am      C  |          D    |Em      |D          |
Come on, come on, set - tle down in - side my love.          Ah.
G       Am      C   |      D      |
Come on, come on, jump  a little higher.
G         Am          C   |      D      |
  Come on, come on, if you feel  a little lighter.
G       Am
Come on, come on,
   C    |          D    |Em    |A    |C        |
We were once upon a time in love.
```

Bridge 2

```
                                  ‖G                 |C
We're accidentally in   love,
                    |Em              |D
Accidentally in   love.
                    |G               |C
Accidentally in   love.
                    |Em              |D
Accidentally in   love.
                    |G               |C
Accidentally in   love.
                    |Em              |D
Accidentally in   love.
                    |G               |C
Accidentally in   love.
                    |Em          |D              ‖
Accidentally in   love.        Accidentally…
```

Bridge 3

```
G                              |C                            |
   I'm in love, I'm in love,   I'm in love, I'm in love,
Em                             |D               |
   I'm in love, I'm in love,     accidentally.
G                              |C                            |
   I'm in love, I'm in love,   I'm in love, I'm in love,
Em                             |D              ‖
   I'm in love, I'm in love,     accidentally.
```

Chorus 3

```
G        Am       C |        D     |
Come on, come on, spin   a little tighter.
G          Am            C    |       D       |
   Come on, come on, and the world's  a little brighter.
G        Am           C  |       D    |Em        |D
Come on, come on, just get yourself in - side her love.
                  |G      ‖
I'm in love.
```

6

Arms of a Woman

Words and Music by
Amos Lee

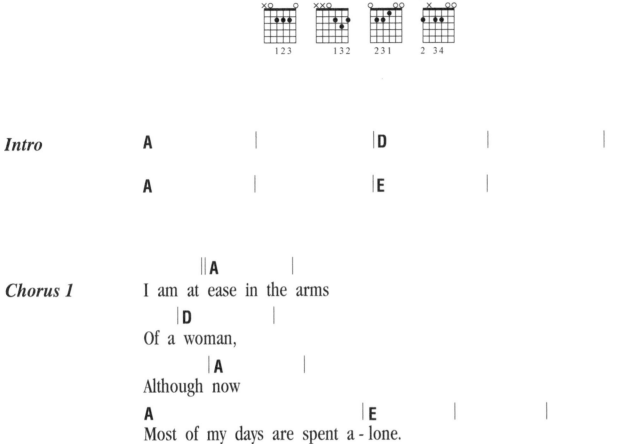

Intro

A | |D | |

A | |E | |

Chorus 1

    ‖A |
I am at ease in the arms
    |D |
Of a woman,
    |A |
Although now

A |E | |
Most of my days are spent a - lone.
F♯m7add4 | |E |
           A thousand miles   from the place I was born,
      |D |E |A |
But when she wakes me, she takes me back home.

Verse 1

‖**A** |

Now most days I spend

 |**D** |

Like a child

   |**A**

Who's a - fraid

  | |**E** | |

Of ghosts in the night.

F♯m7add4 | |**E** |

            I know   there ain't nothing out there.

        |**D** |**E** |**A** |

I'm still   afraid to turn off the light.

Repeat Chorus 1

Interlude   **E** | |**A** | |

                      E | |**A** | ‖

8

Chorus 2

F#m7add4 | |E |
A thousand miles   from the place I was born,

           |D |E |A |
But when she wakes me, she takes me back home.

Chorus 3

       ||A |
I am at ease in the arms

   |D |
Of a woman,

     |A |
Although now

A |E | |
Most of my days are spent a - lone.

F#m7add4 | |E |
A thousand miles   from the place I was born,

     |D |E
But when she wakes me, she takes me,

     |D |E
Yeah, when she wakes me, she takes me,

     |D |E |F#m7add4 |
Yeah, when she wakes me, she takes me back home.

     |D |E |D |A ||
When she wakes me, she takes me back home.

California Dreamin'

Words and Music by
John Phillips and Michelle Phillips

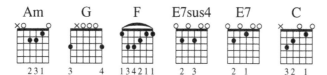

Verse 1

             ||**Am**   **G** |**F**
All the leaves are brown (all the leaves are brown)

        G |**E7sus4** |**E7**
And the sky is grey   (and the sky is grey).

F |**C**   **E7** |**Am**
I've been for a walk (I've been for a walk)

        F |**E7sus4** |**E7**
On a winter's day   (on a winter's day).

          |**Am**   **G** |**F**
I'd be safe and warm (I'd be safe and warm)

        G |**E7sus4** |**E7**
If I was in L.A.   (if I was in L.A.).

        |**Am**   **G** |**F**
California dreamin' (Cali - fornia dream - in')

        G |**E7sus4** |
On such a winter's day.

Verse 2

```
                        ‖Am        G          |F
Stopped in to a church
               G        |E7sus4              |E7
I passed a - long the way.
               F            |C          E7          |Am
Well, I got down on my knees (got down on my knees)
               F        |E7sus4              |E7
And I pre - tend to pray      (I pretend to pray).
                              |Am          G          |F
You know the preacher liked the cold (Preacher liked the cold).
               G        |E7sus4              |E7
He knows I'm gonna stay (knows I'm gonna stay).
               |Am        G        |F
California dreamin' (Cali - fornia dream - in')
       G        |E7sus4          |              ‖
On such a winter's day.
```

Interlude

```
Am                |              |              |F          |

C      E7      |Am      F      |E7sus4      |E7          |

Am      G      |F      G      |E7sus4      |E7              |

Am      G      |F      G      |E7sus4      |E7
```

Verse 3

```
                ‖Am              G                  |F
All the leaves are brown (all the leaves are brown)
          G        |E7sus4                    |E7
And the sky is grey        (and the sky is grey).
F          |C            E7        |Am
I've been for a walk (I've been for a walk)
        F         |E7sus4                  |E7
On a winter's day       (on a winter's day).
              |Am          G        |F
If I didn't tell her (if I didn't tell  her)
        G         |E7sus4                      |E7
I could leave today       (I could leave today).
            |Am          G        |F      G          |Am
California dreamin' (Cali - fornia dream - in') on such a winter's day.
        G        |F        G        |Am
(Cali - fornia dream - in') on such a winter's day.
        G        |F        G          |F        |        |Am       ‖
(Cali - fornia dream - in') on such a winter's day.
```

Daydream

Words and Music by
John Sebastion

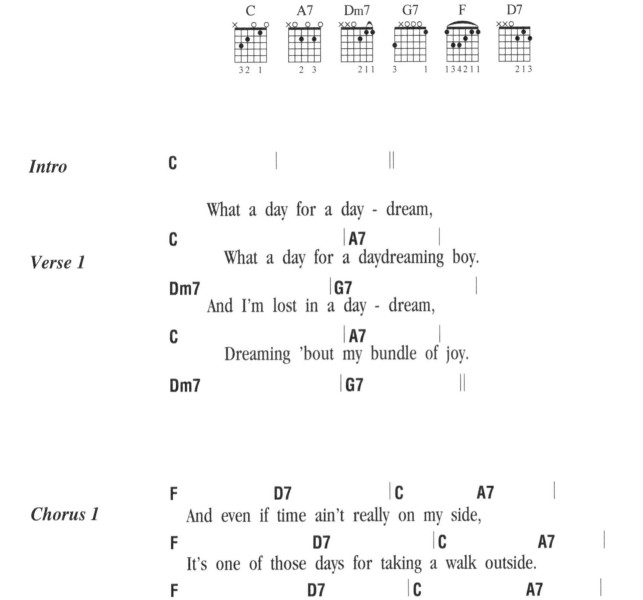

(Capo 1st fret)

Intro

C | ‖

Verse 1

What a day for a day - dream,

C |A7 |
What a day for a daydreaming boy.

Dm7 |G7 |
And I'm lost in a day - dream,

C |A7 |
Dreaming 'bout my bundle of joy.

Dm7 |G7   ‖

Chorus 1

F   D7 |C   A7 |
And even if time ain't really on my side,

F   D7 |C   A7 |
It's one of those days for taking a walk outside.

F   D7 |C   A7 |
I'm blowing the day to take a walk in the sun

Dm7 |G7   ‖
And fall on my face in somebody's new-mowed lawn.

Verse 2

```
C                         |A7            |
    I've been having a sweet   dream;
Dm7                       |G7            |
    I've been dreaming since I woke up today.
C                         |A7            |
    It's starring me in my sweet   dream,
Dm7                       |G7           ||
    'Cause she's the one makes me feel this way.
```

Chorus 2

```
F          D7          |C         A7         |
    And even if time is passing me by a lot,
F          D7          |C           A7       |
    I couldn't care less about the dues you say I got.
F          D7          |C             A7       |
    Tomorrow I'll pay the dues for dropping my load,
Dm7                     |G7              ||
    A pie in the face for being a sleepy bull toad.
```

Interlude

```
C           |A7          |Dm7          |G7              |
Whistle...
C           |A7          |Dm7          |G7             ||
```

Chorus 3

```
F             D7          |C         A7        |
    And you can be sure that if you're feeling right,
F             D7          |C          A7       |
    A daydream will last till along into the night.
F          D7           |C              A7       |
    Tomorrow at breakfast you may pick up your ears,
Dm7                      |G7             ||
    Or you may be daydreaming for a thousand years.
```

Verse 3

```
        C                       |A7              |
        What a day for a day - dream,
        Dm7                     |G7              |
        Custom-made for a daydreaming boy.
        C                       |A7              |
        And I'm lost in a day - dream,
        Dm7                     |G7              ||
        Dreaming 'bout my bundle of joy.
```

Repeat and fade

Outro
```
        ||: F      D7      |C      A7      :||
        Whistle...
```

Different Kind of Fine

Words and Music by
Zac Brown, Wyatt Durrette and Geoffrey Stokes Nielson

(Tune down one half step; low to high: E♭-A♭-D♭-G♭-B♭-E♭)

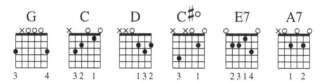

Chorus

‖**G**   **C**
She make a train take a dirt road,

|**G**
Make it stop on a dime.

|**G**   **D**
Make 'em wonder which way to go,

|**G**
Make a man change   his mind.

|**C**   **C#°**
She's a lawyer's queen, a trucker's dream,

|**G**   **E7**
With a baseball hat fit for a queen,

|**A7**   **D** |**G**   ‖
A genuine, a different kind of fine.

Verse 1

G |**C** |
Cadillacs and caviar, well, that ain't how she rolls.

G |**C**   **D**
Implants and tummy tucks, she sure don't need those.

|**G** |
She's a cool drink of water when the summer's mean,

C
Poured into those Levi jeans.

|**G**   **D** |**G**
She's country as the   day is long.

Repeat Chorus

Verse 2

         G
Tan and lean like a long-neck bottle,

      |**C**
In the passenger seat got her hand on the throttle.

    |**G** |**D**
She'll get you there right on time.

    |**G** |
Lord, take you down to Tijuana, make you wanna slap your momma,

C |
Got you all torn up, made you spill your dip cup.

G   **D** |**G**
Bona fide, a different kind of fine.

Repeat Chorus (2x)

Don't Think Twice, It's All Right

Words and Music by Bob Dylan

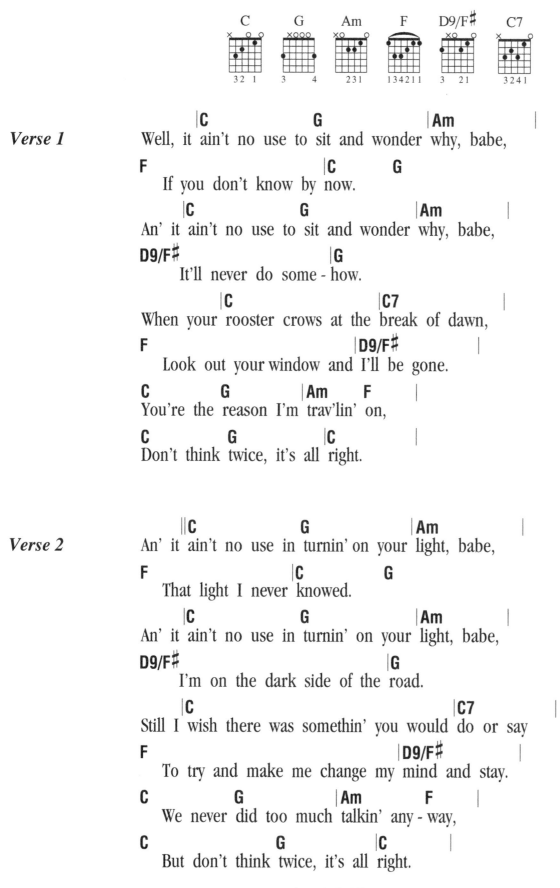

Verse 1

|C   G |Am
Well, it ain't no use to sit and wonder why, babe,

F |C   G
If you don't know by now.

|C   G |Am
An' it ain't no use to sit and wonder why, babe,

D9/F♯ |G
It'll never do some - how.

|C |C7
When your rooster crows at the break of dawn,

F |D9/F♯
Look out your window and I'll be gone.

C   G |Am   F
You're the reason I'm trav'lin' on,

C   G |C
Don't think twice, it's all right.

Verse 2

‖C   G |Am
An' it ain't no use in turnin' on your light, babe,

F |C   G
That light I never knowed.

|C   G |Am
An' it ain't no use in turnin' on your light, babe,

D9/F♯ |G
I'm on the dark side of the road.

|C |C7
Still I wish there was somethin' you would do or say

F |D9/F♯
To try and make me change my mind and stay.

C   G |Am   F
We never did too much talkin' any - way,

C   G |C
But don't think twice, it's all right.

Verse 3

```
      ‖C              G            |Am                  |
     So it ain't no use in callin' out my name, gal,
 F                             |C        G
     Like you never done be - fore.
         |C              G            |Am                  |
     An' it ain't no use in callin' out my name, gal,
 D9/F♯                              |G
     I can't hear you any more.
         |C                      |C7
     I'm a - thinkin' and a - wond'rin' walking down the road,
      |F                    |D9/F♯
     I once loved a woman, a child I'm told.
      |C         G            |Am           F              |
     I give her my heart but she wanted my soul,
 C              G            |C            |
     But don't think twice, it's all right.
```

Verse 4

```
      ‖C   G       |Am
     So long,  honey bee,
             |F              |C       G
     Where I'm bound, I can't tell.
 C         G            |Am           |
     Goodbye is too good a word, gal,
 D9/F♯                              |G            |
     So I'll just say fare - thee - well.
 C                     |C7
     I ain't sayin' you treated me unkind,
      |F                      |D9/F♯               |
     You could have done better but I don't mind.
 C         G           |Am           F           |
     You just  kinda wasted my precious time,
 C              G            |C            ‖
     But don't think twice, it's all right.
```

Eight Days a Week

Words and Music by
John Lennon and Paul McCartney

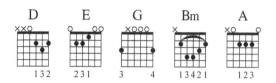

D	E	G	Bm	A
1 3 2	2 3 1	3 4	1 3 4 2 1	1 2 3

Intro   D |E |G |D   ‖

Verse 1

D |E |
Ooh, I need your love, babe;
G |D |
Guess you know it's true.
D |E |
Hope you need my love, babe,
G |D   ‖
Just like I need you.

Chorus

Bm |G |
Hold me, love me,
Bm |E |
Hold me, love me.
 |D |E |
I ain't got nothing but love, babe,
G |D   ‖
Eight days a week.

Verse 2

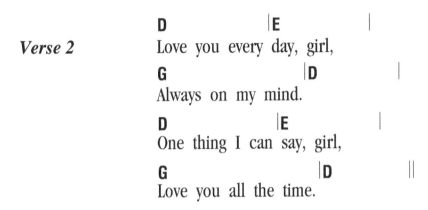

D |**E** |
Love you every day, girl,

G |**D** |
Always on my mind.

D |**E** |
One thing I can say, girl,

G |**D** ||
Love you all the time.

Repeat Chorus

Bridge

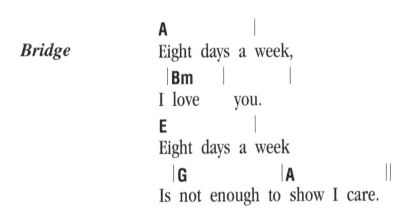

A |
Eight days a week,

|**Bm** | |
I love   you.

E |
Eight days a week

|**G** |**A** ||
Is not enough to show I care.

Repeat Verse 1

Repeat Chorus

Repeat Bridge

Repeat Verse 2

Repeat Chorus

G |**D** |
Eight days a week.

G |**D**   ‖
Eight days a week.

Outro   **D** |**E** |**G** |**D**   ‖

I'm Yours

Words and Music by
Jason Mraz

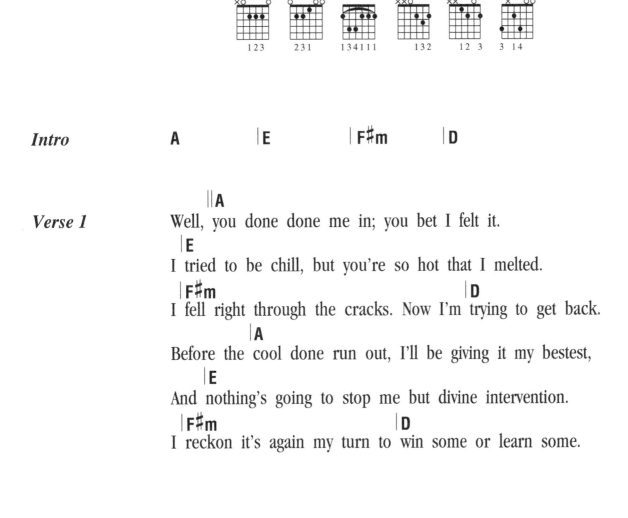

(Capo 2nd fret)

A   E   F#m   D   B7/D#   E/G#

Intro
    A |**E** |**F#m** |**D**

Verse 1

        ‖**A**
Well, you done done me in; you bet I felt it.
   |**E**
I tried to be chill, but you're so hot that I melted.
 |**F#m** |**D**
I fell right through the cracks. Now I'm trying to get back.
             |**A**
Before the cool done run out, I'll be giving it my bestest,
       |**E**
And nothing's going to stop me but divine intervention.
 |**F#m** |**D**
I reckon it's again my turn to win some or learn some.

Chorus 1

      ‖**A** |**E** |**F#m**
But I won't hesi - tate no more, no more.
        |**D**   **A**
It cannot wait. I'm yours.
    |**E** |**F#m** |**D**   ‖
Mm,   mm, hmm, mm.

Verse 2

              A   **|E**

Well, open up your mind and see like me.

                                        |F♯m

Open up your plans and, damn, you're free.

                              |D   **|**

Look into your heart and you'll find love, love, love, love.

A   **E**

Listen to the music of the moment; people dance and   sing.

                        |F♯m

We're just one big family.

                                        |D   **|B7/D♯**

And it's our god-forsaken right to be loved,   loved, loved, loved, loved.

Chorus 2

             ||A   **|E**   **|F♯m**

So, I won't hesi‑tate no more, no more.

             |D

It cannot wait. I'm sure.

             |A   **|E**

There's no need to compli‑cate.

            |F♯m

Our time is short.

            |D   **||**

This is our fate. I'm yours.

Interlude

A   **E/G♯** **|F♯m**   **E**

Scat sing...

                        |D   **|B7/D♯**   **|**

Skooch on over closer, dear,   and I will nibble your ear.   *Scat sing...*

A   **E/G♯** **|F♯m**   **E**   **|D**   **|B7/D♯**

Verse 3

|| A

I've been spending way too long checking my tongue in the mirror

| E

And bending over backwards just to try to see it clearer.

| F♯m | D

But my breath fogged up the glass, and so I drew a new face and I laughed.

| A

I guess what I'll be saying is there ain't no better reason

| E

To rid yourself of vanities and just go with the seasons.

| F♯m | D

It's   what we aim to do. Our name is our virtue.

Chorus 3

|| A | E | F♯m

But I won't hesi‑tate no more, no more.

          | D |

It cannot wait. I'm yours.

A | E

Open up your mind and see like me.

                                | F♯m

Open up your plans and, damn, you're free.

                         | D

Look into your heart and you'll find that   the sky is yours.

      | A

So please don't, please don't, please don't...

           | E | F♯m

There's no need to complicate 'cause our time   is short.

             | D | B7/D♯ ||

This is, this is, this is our fate. I'm yours.

Outro   A | E | F♯m | D | A ||

Scat sing...

Forever Young

Words and Music by
Bob Dylan

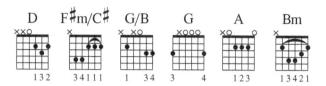

Verse 1

‖**D**
May God bless and keep you always,
|**F♯m/C♯**
May your wishes all come true,
|**G/B**
May you always do for others
|**G** |**D** |
And let others do for you.
|**D**
May you build a ladder to the stars
|**F♯m/C♯** |**G/B** |**A**
And climb on every rung, may you stay
|**D** |
Forever young.

Chorus

‖**A** | |**Bm** |
Forever young,   forever young,
|**D** |**A** |**D** |
May you stay   forever young.

Verse 2

```
              ‖D
May you grow up to be righteous,
         |F♯m/C♯
May you grow up to be true,
         |G/B
May you always know the truth
             |G                    |D            |
And see the lights surrounding you.
             |D
May you always be courageous,
             |F♯m/C♯                        |G/B       |A
Stand up - right and be strong, and may you stay
             |D            |
Forever young.
```

Repeat Chorus

Verse 3

```
              ‖D
May your hands always be busy,
         |F♯m/C♯
May your feet always be swift,
         |G/B
May you have a strong foundation
             |G                    |D            |
When the winds of changes shift.
             |D
May your heart always be joyful,
             |F♯m/C♯                     |G/B       |A
May your song always be sung, and may you stay
             |D            |
Forever young.
```

Repeat Chorus

Gravity

Words and Music by
John Mayer

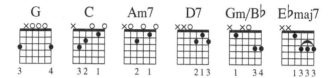

Intro   **G** | |**C** | |**G** | |**C** | ||

Verse 1

G |
Gravity

   |**C** |
Is working a - gainst me,

   |**G** |
And gravity

   |**C** |
Wants to bring me down.

Chorus 1

   ||**Am7** |
Oh, I'll never know what makes this man,

   |**D7** | |
With all the love that his heart can stand,

Gm/B♭
Dream of ways

   |**E♭maj7** |**D7** | ||
To throw it all away.   Woh, woh.

Repeat Verse 1

Chorus 2

‖**Am7**
Oh, twice as much ain't twice as good

|**D7**
And can't sustain like one-half could.

|**Gm/B♭**
It's wanting more

|**E♭maj7** |**D7**
That's gonna send me to my knees.

Interlude   **G** | |**C** | |**G** | |**C** |

Repeat Chorus 2

Verse 2

‖**G**
Woh, woh. Gravity,

|**C**
Stay the hell a - way from me.

|**G**
Woh, woh. Gravity

|**C**
Has taken better men   than me.   How can that be?

Outro

‖**G**
Just keep me where the light is.

|**C**
Just keep me where the light is.

|**G**
Just keep me where the light is.

|**C** | |**G**
Come on, keep me where the light is.

The Heart of Life

Words and Music by
John Mayer

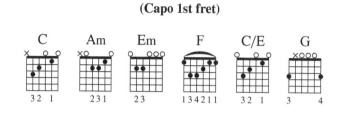

(Capo 1st fret)

Intro

| C | | |Am | | |Em |F |C/E |G | ‖ |

Verse 1

C | |Am |
I   hate to see you cry,

Am |Em |F |C/E |G |
Lying there in that po - si - tion.

C | |Am |
There's   things you need to hear,

Am |Em |F |C/E |G ‖
So turn off your tears   and   lis - ten.

Chorus 1

G |C |F | |
Pain throws your heart to the ground.

G |C |F | |
Love turns the whole thing a - round.

G |C |F |C/E
No, it won't all go the way it should,

|F |C/E |G |C | ‖
But I know the heart of life is good.

Repeat Intro

Verse 2

```
          C        |              |Am       |
          You   know, it's nothing new.
          Am           |Em   |F   |C/E   |G
          Bad news never had    good    tim  -  ing.
             |C       |          |Am       |
          But then,  the circle of your friends
          Am           |Em   |F   |C/E   |G        ||
          Will defend the sil  -  ver    lin  -  ing.
```

Repeat Chorus 1

Repeat Intro (2x)

Chorus 2

```
          G                    |C           |F       |       |
          Pain throws your heart   to the ground.
          G                    |C         |F     |       |
          Love turns the whole     thing around.
          G      |C           |F    |C/E
          Fear is a friend who's mis - under - stood,
             |F     |C/E   |F   |C/E
          But I know the heart of life is good.
           |G       |     |     ||
          I know it's good.
```

I Can't Help But Wonder (Where I'm Bound)

Words and Music by Tom Paxton

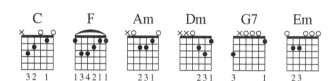

Verse 1

| |C | | |F | Am |Dm
It's a long and dusty road, it's a hot and a heavy load,

|G7 | |C |
And the folks I meet ain't always kind.

|C |
Some are bad and some are good,

|F Am |Dm
Some have done the best they could,

|G7 | |C |
Some have tried to ease my troublin' mind.

Chorus

‖Dm |G7
And I can't help but wonder

|C Em |Am
Where I'm bound, where I'm bound.

Dm |G7 |C |
Can't help but wonder where I'm bound.

Verse 2

‖C | |F Am |Dm
I have wandered through this land just a - doin' the best I can,

|G7 | |C |
Tryin' to find what I was meant to do.

|C | |F Am |Dm
And the people that I see look as worried as can be

|G7 | |C |
And it looks like they are wonderin', too.

Repeat Chorus

Verse 3

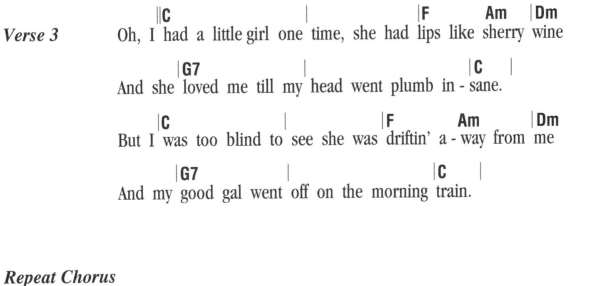

     ‖C | |F   Am |Dm
Oh, I had a little girl one time, she had lips like sherry wine

     |G7 | |C |
And she loved me till my head went plumb in - sane.

     |C | |F   Am |Dm
But I was too blind to see she was driftin' a - way from me

     |G7 | |C |
And my good gal went off on the morning train.

Repeat Chorus

Verse 4

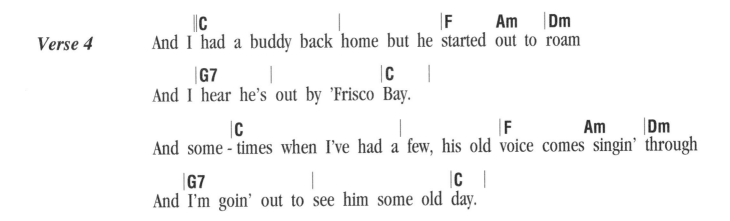

     ‖C | |F   Am |Dm
And I had a buddy back home but he started out to roam

     |G7 | |C |
And I hear he's out by 'Frisco Bay.

     |C | |F   Am |Dm
And some - times when I've had a few, his old voice comes singin' through

     |G7 | |C |
And I'm goin' out to see him some old day.

Repeat Chorus

Verse 5

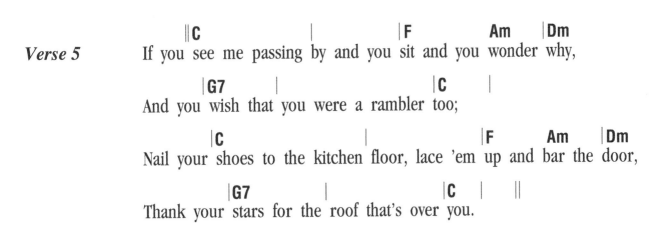

     ‖C | |F   Am |Dm
If you see me passing by and you sit and you wonder why,

     |G7 | |C |
And you wish that you were a rambler too;

     |C | |F   Am |Dm
Nail your shoes to the kitchen floor, lace 'em up and bar the door,

     |G7 | |C | ‖
Thank your stars for the roof that's over you.

I Should Have Known Better

Words and Music by
John Lennon and Paul McCartney

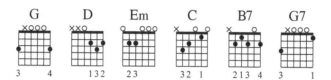

Intro   G   D |G   D |G   D |G   D ||

Verse 1

G D |G D |
I   should have known
G   D |G D
Better with a girl like you
      |G   D |Em
That I would love every - thing that you do;
     |C |D |G D |G
And I do, hey, hey, hey,   and I do.

Verse 2

D ||G D |G
Woh, woh, I
D |G   D |G D
Never real - ized what a kiss could be;
  |G   D |Em
This could only happen to me.
         |C |B7 ||
Can't you see, can't you see

Bridge

```
Em              |C                    |G        |B7       |
    That when I tell you that I love  you, oh,
Em                        |                |G   |G7       |
    You're gonna say  you love me too,            oh.
C           |D                  |G      |Em       |
    And when I ask you  to be mine,
C                    |D                  |G  D  |G
    You're gonna say  you love me too.
```

Verse 3

```
D ‖G  D  |G
So I
D                   |G            D          |G  D
Should have real - ized a lot of things before.
        |G            D            |Em
If this is love, you got to give me more;
            |C                 |D
Give me more,  hey, hey, hey,
            |G    D   |G    D      ‖
Give me more.
```

Interlude

```
G    D    |G    D    |G    D    |G    D    |G    D       |

Em          |C           |D           |G  D  |G
```

Repeat Verse 2

Repeat Bridge

Outro

Repeat and fade

```
    D              ‖:G  D    |G   D           :‖
You love me, too.                  You love me, too.
```

I Want to Know What Love Is

Words and Music by
Mick Jones

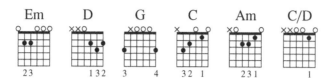

Verse 1

      Em   **D**   **|G**
     I've gotta take a lit - tle time,

       |C   **|Em**   **|**   **|**
A little time to think things over.

      Em   **D**   **|G**
     I better read between the lines,

      |C   **|Em**   **|**   **|D** **|Em**   **|**   **||**
In case I need it when I'm old - er.

Verse 2

      Em   **D**   **|G**
     Now, this mountain I must climb

       |C   **|Em**   **|**
Feels like the world upon my shoul - ders.

      Em   **D**   **|G**
     Through the clouds I see love shine,

       |C   **|Em**   **|**
It keeps me warm as life grows colder.

Pre-Chorus

‖C Am |D   Am |

In my life   there's been heartache and pain.

C   Am |D   Am |

I don't know if I can face it again.

C   Am |D   Am

Can't stop now, I've traveled so far

|C   G   Am G C/D | ‖

To change this lone-ly life.

Chorus

G   Em |D |

I want to know what love is.

Am   Em |D |

I want you to show me.

G   Em |D |

I want to feel what love is.

Am   Em |D | |Em | ‖

I know you can show me.

Verse 3

Em   D |G

I'm gonna take a lit - tle time,

|C |Em |

A little time to look around me.

Em   D |G

I've got nowhere left to hide,

|C |Em |

It looks like love has finally found me.

Repeat Pre-Chorus

Repeat Chorus (2X)

I've Just Seen a Face

Words and Music by
John Lennon and Paul McCartney

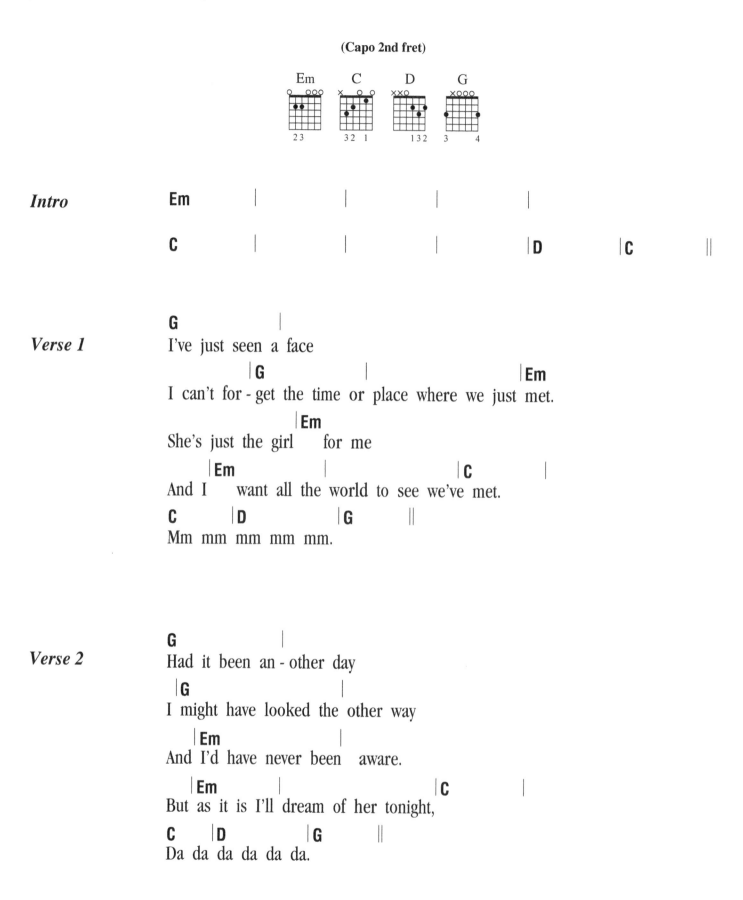

(Capo 2nd fret)

Em   C   D   G

Intro

Em | | | |

C | | | |**D** |**C** ||

Verse 1

G |
I've just seen a face
|**G** | |**Em**
I can't for - get the time or place where we just met.
|**Em**
She's just the girl   for me
|**Em** | |**C** |
And I   want all the world to see we've met.
C |**D** |**G** ||
Mm mm mm mm mm.

Verse 2

G |
Had it been an - other day
|**G** |
I might have looked the other way
|**Em** |
And I'd have never been   aware.
|**Em** | |**C** |
But as it is I'll dream of her tonight,
C |**D** |**G** ||
Da da da da da da.

Chorus

```
        D          |
Falling,
              | C        |
Yes, I am falling,
                  | G        |
And she keeps calling
C             | G      |        ||
   Me back a - gain.
```

Verse 3

```
G              |                    |
I have never known the like of this;
                  | G           |
I've been a - lone and I have
Em                        |
Missed things and kept out of sight.
    | Em          |              | C        |
But other girls were never quite like this,
C    | D         | G        ||
Da da da da da da.
```

Repeat Chorus

Interlude

```
G          |          |          | Em        |          |

Em         |      | C        |        | D      | G        ||
```

Repeat Chorus

Repeat Verse 1

Repeat Chorus (3x)

It Ain't Me Babe

Words and Music by
Bob Dylan

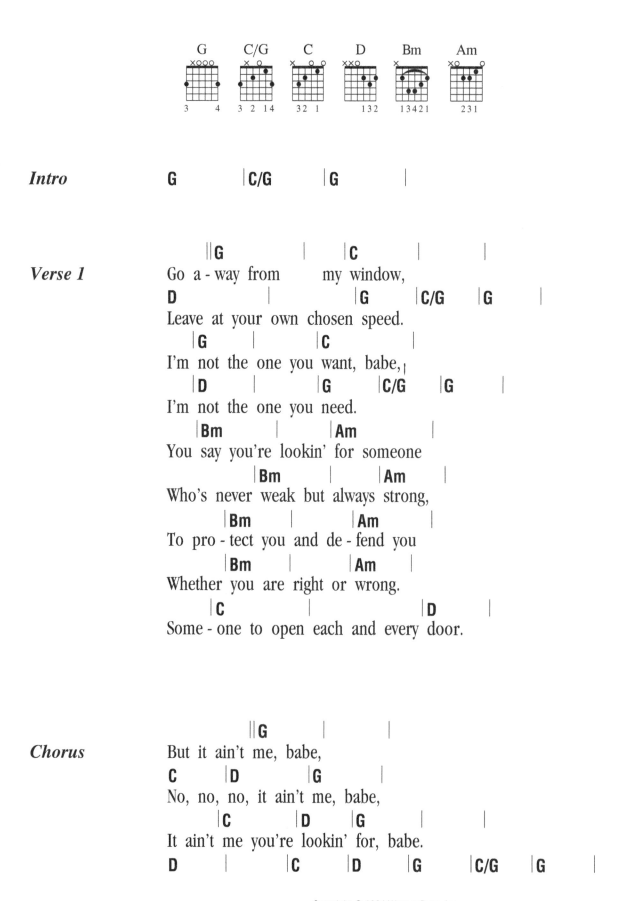

Intro   G |C/G |G |

Verse 1
‖G | |C | |
Go a - way from   my window,
D | |G |C/G |G |
Leave at your own chosen speed.
|G | |C |
I'm not the one you want, babe,
|D | |G |C/G |G |
I'm not the one you need.
|Bm | |Am |
You say you're lookin' for someone
|Bm | |Am |
Who's never weak but always strong,
|Bm | |Am |
To pro - tect you and de - fend you
|Bm | |Am |
Whether you are right or wrong.
|C | | |D |
Some - one to open each and every door.

Chorus
‖G | | |
But it ain't me, babe,
C |D |G |
No, no, no, it ain't me, babe,
|C |D |G | |
It ain't me you're lookin' for, babe.
D | |C |D |G |C/G |G |

Verse 2

```
       ‖G        |          |C            |
       Go  lightly      from  the  ledge,  babe,
         |D        |        |G      |C/G     |G         |
       Go  lightly  on  the  ground.
          |G        |        |C            |
       I'm  not  the  one  you  want,  babe,
          |D   |        |G      |C/G     |G          |
       I'll  only  let  you  down.
           |Bm        |        |Am           |
       You  say  you're  lookin'  for  someone
             |Bm        |        |Am         |
       Who'll  promise  never  to  part,
             |Bm     |        |Am            |
       Some - one  to  close  his  eyes  for  you,
             |Bm        |        |Am         |
       Some - one  to  close  his  heart,
          |C            |                |D        |
       Some - one  who  will  die  for  you  and  more.
```

Repeat Chorus

Verse 3

```
 ‖G          |     |C     |        |
Go  melt  back  in  the  night;
 D              |            |G     |C/G   |G     |
Everything  in - side  is  made  of  stone.
       |G     |       |C     |
There's  nothing  in  here  moving
   |D     |        |G     |C/G   |G        |
And  anyway  I'm  not  a - lone.
 |Bm           |     |Am       |
You  say  you're  lookin'  for  someone
            |Bm          |     |Am       |
Who'll  pick  you  up  each  time  you  fall,
 |Bm     |        |Am       |
To  gather  flowers  constantly,
       |Bm          |     |Am       |
And  to  come  each  time  you  call,
 |C           |            |D        |
A  lover  for  your  life  and  nothin'  more.
```

Chorus

```
            ‖G        |        |
But  it  ain't  me,  babe,
C     |D         |G        |
No,  no,  no,  it  ain't  me,  babe,
      |C        |D     |G     |        |
It  ain't  me  you're  lookin'  for,  babe.
D        |        |C     |          |D     |          |G     |C/G   |G     |‖
```

Make This Day

Words and Music by
Zac Brown, Wyatt Durrette, Nic Cowan, Coy Bowles, Clay Cook, Jimmy De Martini, Chris Fryar and John Driskell Hopkins

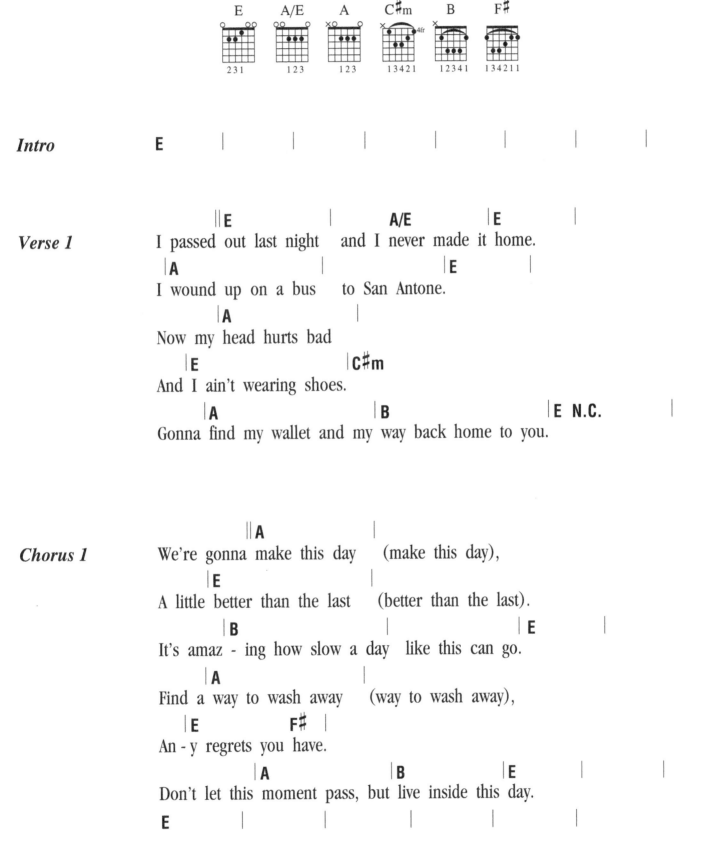

Verse 2

```
    ‖E                    |  A/E          |E            |
I got cuffs on my hands,    chains on my feet.
   |A                    |                 |E            |
I got locked up for the second time this week.
      |A                 |
And I know I make you cry,
      |E            |C♯m
But girl my love is true.
         |A                    |B              |E N.C.        |
I'm gonna find my wallet and my way back home to you.
```

Chorus 2

```
            ‖A            |
We're gonna make this day   (make this day),
      |E               |
A little better than the last    (better than the last).
         |B            |                |E            |
It's amaz - ing how slow a day  like this can pass.
      |A              |
Find a way to wash away    (way to wash away),
    |E            F♯ |
An - y regrets you have.
         |A          |B          |E          |
Don't let this moment pass, but live inside this day.
```

Verse 3

```
        ‖E              |  A/E        |E          |            |
Now I'm back on the street,    thumb in the air.
A                      |                 |E          |
Don't know how the hell   that I got here.
        |A                |
But I'm gonna hitch that ride
         |E            |C♯m
If it's the last thing I do.
         |A              |B            |E N.C.        |
I'm gonna find that wallet and bring it home to you.
```

Repeat Chorus 2

Chorus 3

           ‖**A** |
We're gonna make this day   (make this day),

       |**E** |
A little better than the last   (better than the last).

          |**B** | |**N.C.** |
Oh, now, don't you let this life come whip your...

       |**A** |
Find a way to wash away   (way to wash away),

     |**E**   **F♯** |
An - y regrets you have.

           |**A** |**B** |**E** | ‖
Don't let this moment pass, but live inside this day.

Just the Two of Us

Words and Music by
Ralph MacDonald, William Salter and Bill Withers

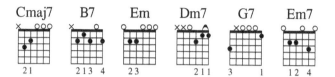

Verse 1

Cmaj7   **B7**   **|Em**
I see the crystal raindrops fall,

Dm7 **G7** **|Cmaj7**
And the beauty of it all

B7   **|Em7**   **|**
Is when the sun comes shining through

Cmaj7   **B7**   **|Em**
To make those rainbows in my mind

Dm7 **G7**   **|Cmaj7**
When I think of you some-time,

B7   **|Em**
And I want to spend some time with you.

Chorus

‖Cmaj7   **B7**   **|Em7**   **Dm7**
Just the two of us, we can make it if we try.

G7 **|Cmaj7** **B7**   **|Em**
Just the two of us. (Just the two of us.)

|Cmaj7   **B7**   **|Em7**   **Dm7**
Just the two of us building castles in the sky.

G7 **|Cmaj7** **B7**   **|Em7**   **‖**
Just the two of us, you and I.

Verse 2

```
Cmaj7                  B7               |Em
      We look for love, no time for tears.

        Dm7    G7       |Cmaj7
Wasted  water's  all  that  is

            B7                   |Em7      |
And  it  don't  make  no  flowers  grow.

Cmaj7                    B7                 |Em
      Good  things  might  come  to  those  who  wait,

        Dm7      G7        |Cmaj7
But  not  for  those  who  wait  too  late.

            B7           |Em
We've  got  to  go    for  all  we  know.
```

Repeat Chorus

Verse 3

```
Cmaj7             B7             |Em
      I  hear  the  crystal  raindrops  fall

        Dm7    G7        |Cmaj7
On  the  window  down  the  hall

          B7                   |Em7      |
And  it  be-comes  the  morning  dew.

Cmaj7                 B7                 |Em
      And,  darling,  when  the  morning  comes

        Dm7    G7       |Cmaj7
And  I  see  the  morning  sun,

            B7               |Em
I  want  to  be    the  one  with  you.
```

Repeat Chorus (2X)

The Letter

Words and Music by
Wayne Carson Thompson

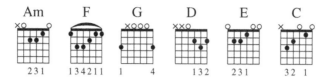

Verse 1

Am   **|F** |
Give me a ticket for an aeroplane.
G   **|D** |
Ain't got time to take a fast train.
Am |
Lonely days are gone,
F
I'm a-goin' home.
     |E   **|Am** ||
My baby just wrote me a letter.

Verse 2

Am   **|F** |
I don't care how much money I gotta spend.
G   **|D** |
Got to get back to my baby again.
Am |
Lonely days are gone,
F
I'm a-goin' home.
     |E   **|Am** |
My baby just wrote me a letter.

Bridge

     ||**C**   **G**
Well, she wrote me a let - ter,
      |**F**   **C** |**G** | |
Said she couldn't live without me no more.
C   **G**
Listen to me, mister, can't you see
 |**F**   **C** |**G** |
I got to get back to my baby once more?
E ||
  Anyway...

Repeat Verse 1

Repeat Bridge

Verse 3

  Am |**F** |
Give me a ticket for an aeroplane.
G |**D** |
Ain't got time to take a fast train.
Am |
Lonely days are gone,
F
I'm a-goin' home.
 |**E** |**Am**
My baby just wrote me a letter.
 |**E** |**Am** ||
My baby just wrote me a letter.

Life Is Wonderful

Words and Music by
Jason Mraz

(Tune down one half step; low to high: E♭-A♭-D♭-G♭-B♭-E♭)

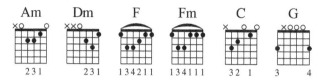

Am   Dm   F   Fm   C   G

   2 3 1   2 3 1   1 3 4 2 1 1   1 3 4 1 1 1   3 2 1   3   4

Verse 1

‖**Am** |
It takes a crane to build   a crane.
|**Dm** |
It takes two floors to make a   story.
|**F**
It takes an egg to make a hen.
|**Fm**
It takes a hen to make an egg.
|**C** |**G**
There is no end to what I'm   saying.

Verse 2

‖**Am** |
It takes a thought to make   a word.
|**Dm** |
And it takes some words to make an   action.
|**F**
And it takes some work to make it work.
|**Fm**
It takes some good to make it hurt.
|**C** |**G** ‖
It takes some bad for satis - faction.

Chorus 1

```
Am                            |Dm                  |
Ah, la, la, la, la, la, la. Life    is wonderful.
G                          |C                      |
Ah, la, la, la, la, la, la. Life    goes full circle.
Am                          |Dm                    |
   Ah, la, la, la, la. Life    is wonderful.
G                     |              |Am         |        |        |
Ah, la, la, la, la.           Mm.
```

Verse 3

```
                              ||Am                |
It takes a night to make it    dawn.
                              |Dm                     |
And it takes a day to make you yawn, brother.
                              |F
And it takes some old to make you young.
                              |F
It takes some cold to know the sun.
                              |C                    |G
It takes the one to have    the other.
```

Verse 4

```
                              ||Am                 |
And it takes no time to fall in love.
                              |Dm                     |
But it takes you years to know what love is.
                              |F
And it takes some fears to make you trust.
                              |F
It takes those tears to make it rust.
                              |C              |G          ||
It takes the dust to have it pol - ished.    Yeah.
```

Chorus 2

```
Am                         |Dm                |
Ah, la, la, la, la, la. Life   is wonderful.
  G                          |C              |
  Ah, la, la, la, la, la. Life   goes full circle.
  Am                         |Dm              |
  Ah, la, la, la, la, la. Life   is wonderful.
  G                 |          |Am       |          |          |
  Ah, la, la, la.        It is,   it is so ...
          |Am             |          |          |
And it is    so ...
```

Verse 5

```
                              ‖Am               |
It takes some silence to make sound.
                            |Dm              |
And it takes a loss before you found it.
                         |F
And it takes a road to go no - where.
                          |Fm
It takes a toll to make you care.
                    |C                |G              ‖
It takes a hole to make a mountain.
```

Chorus 3

```
Am                         |Dm              |
Ah, la, la, la, la, la. Life   is wonderful.
  G                        |C              |
  Ah, la, la, la, la, la. Life   goes full circle.
  Am                       |Dm              |
  Ah, la, la, la, la, la. Life   is wonderful.
  G                        |C              |
  Ah, la, la, la, la, la. Life   is meaningful.
  Am                         |Dm              |
  Ah, la, la, la, la, la, la, la. Life is wonderful.
  G                          |
  Ah, la, la, la, la, la.
```

Outro

|| **Am** | | |

It is   so   wonder - ful.

| **Am** |

And it is   so meaning - ful.

| **Am** |

It is   so wonder - ful.

| **Am** | | ||

It is   meaning - ful.

Like a Rolling Stone

Words and Music by
Bob Dylan

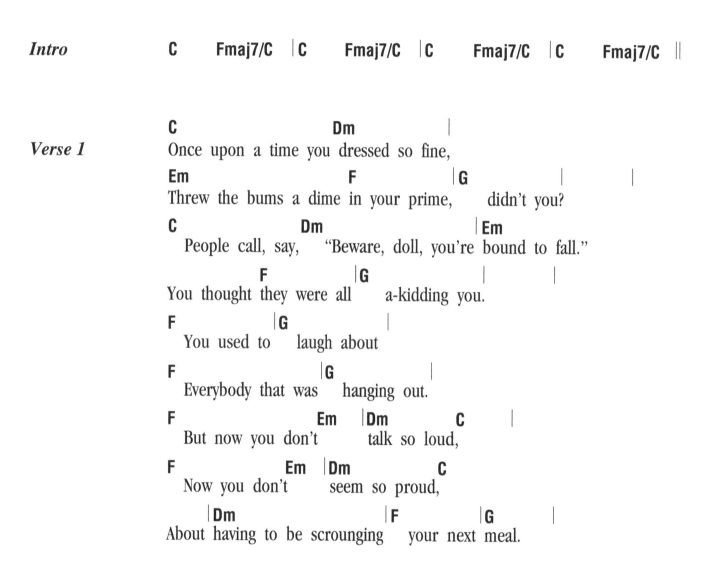

Intro   C   Fmaj7/C |C   Fmaj7/C |C   Fmaj7/C |C   Fmaj7/C ‖

Verse 1

C   Dm |
Once upon a time you dressed so fine,

Em   F |G | |
Threw the bums a dime in your prime,   didn't you?

C   Dm |Em
    People call, say,   "Beware, doll, you're bound to fall."

              F |G | |
You thought they were all   a-kidding you.

F |G |
You used to   laugh about

F |G |
Everybody that was   hanging out.

F   Em |Dm   C |
But now you don't   talk so loud,

F   Em |Dm   C
Now you don't   seem so proud,

    |Dm |F |G |
About having to be scrounging   your next meal.

Chorus 1

              ‖**C**   **F** |**G**
How does it feel?

            |**C**   **F** |**G**
How does it feel

              |**C**   **F** |**G**
To be without a home,

           |**C**   **F** |**G**
Like a complete un - known,

            |**C**   **F** |**G** |**C** **F** |**G** |
Like a rolling stone?

Verse 2

            ‖**C**   **Dm**
Oh, you've gone to the finest school,

 |**Em**   **F** |**G** |
Al - right, Miss Lonely, but you know you only used to get   juiced in it.

 |**C**   **Dm** |**Em**
No - body's ever taught you how to live out on the street,

          F |**G** | |
And now you're gonna have to get   used to it.

F |**G** |
  You say you never   compromise

F |**G** |
  With the mystery tramp, but now you   realize

F   **Em** |**Dm**   **C** |
  He's not selling any   alibis

F   **Em** |**Dm**   **C**
As you stare into the vacuum of his eyes

 |**Dm** |**F** |**G** |
And say, "Do you want to   make a deal?"

Chorus 2

```
                    ‖C    F    |G
How does it feel?
                     |C    F    |G
How does it feel
                       |C    F    |G
To be on your own,
                        |C      F    |G
With no direction home,
                       |C    F    |G
A complete unknown,
                       |C    F    |G          |C    F    |G          |
Like a rolling stone?
```

Verse 3

```
              ‖C               Dm                    |
Oh, you   never turned a - round to see the frowns
Em                      F                      |G          |          |
    On the jugglers and the clowns when they all did     tricks for you.
C                      Dm
Never understood that it ain't no good,
    |Em              F              |G          |          |
You shouldn't let other people get your     kicks for you.
F                                          |G          |
    You used to ride on a chrome horse with your     diplomat
F                        |G          |
    Who carried on his shoulder a     Siamese cat.
F          Em          |Dm     C    |
    Ain't it hard    when you dis - cover that
F          Em     |Dm          C      |
    He really wasn't    where it's at
Dm                        |          F          |G          |
After he took from you everything   he could steal.
```

```
          ‖C    F    |G
How does it feel?
          |C    F    |G
How does it feel
            |C    F    |G
To have you on your own,
              |C     F    |G
With no direction home,
               |C      F    |G
Like a complete unknown,
              |C   F   |G        |C  F   |G        |
Like a rolling stone?
```

Verse 4

```
     ‖C              Dm                |
Oh,     princess on the steeple and all the
Em                  F                        |G        |       |
Pretty people, they're all drinking, thinking that they've    got it made,
C            Dm                |
  Exchanging all   precious gifts,
Em                 F                     |G                      |     |
   But you'd better take your diamond ring,   you'd better pawn it, babe.
F           |G       |
  You used to be   so amused
F                |G                              |
   At Napoleon in rags   and the language that he used.
F                Em            |Dm   C    |
  Go to him now, he calls you, you can't    refuse.
F                  Em          |Dm           C    |
When you ain't got nothing,   you've got   nothing to lose.
Dm                            |    F    |G      |
   You're invisible now, you've got no secrets  to con - ceal.
```

Repeat Chorus 2

Me and Julio Down by the Schoolyard

Words and Music by
Paul Simon

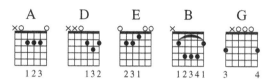

Intro A D A| E |A D A| E

Verse 1

    ||**A** |
The mama pajama rolled   out of bed
    |**A** |**D** |
And she ran to the police sta - tion.
    |**E** |
When the papa found out, he be - gan to shout,
    |**E** |**A** |
And he started the investiga - tion.

Bridge

A Tacet ||**E** |
    It's against the law;
    |**A** |
It was against the law.
    |**E** |
What the mama saw,
    |**A** |
It was against the law.

Verse 2

‖**A** |
The mama looked down and spit on the ground

|**A** |**D** |
Every time my name gets men - tioned,

|**E** |
The papa said, "Oy, if I get that boy,

|**E** |**A** |
I'm gonna stick him in the house of deten - tion"

Chorus

A Tacet ‖**D** |
Well, I'm on my way;

|**A** |
I don't know where I'm goin'.

|**D** |
I'm on my way;

|**A** **B** |**E**
I'm taking my time but I don't know where.

|**D** | **G** |**A** |
Goodbye to Ro - sie, the Queen of Coro - na.

|**A** **G** |**D** **E** |**A** **D** **A**| **E**
See you, me and Julio down by the schoolyard.

|**A** **G** |**D** **E** |**A** **D** **A**| **E**
See you, me and Julio down by the schoolyard.

Verse 3

‖**A** |
In a couple of days they come and take me away,

|**A** |**D** |
But the press let the story leak.

|**E** |
And when the radical priest come to get me released,

|**E** |**A** |
We's all on the cover of *News - week*.

Repeat Chorus

|A   G |D   E |A   D A| E   ‖

See you, me and Julio down by the schoolyard.

Outro   A   D   A| E |A   D   A| E |

                A   D   A| E |A   D   A| E |A   ‖

Never Say Goodbye

Words and Music by
Jon Bon Jovi and Richie Sambora

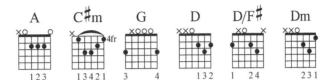

Verse 1

A
As I sit in this smoky room,

C♯m
The night about to end,

G
I pass my time with strangers,

|D
But this bottle's my only friend.

A
Remember when we used to park

|C♯m
On   Butler Street out in the dark?

G
Remember when we lost the keys

|D
And   you lost more than that in my backseat? Believe it.

A
Remember how we used to talk

|C♯m
About   busting out? We'd break their hearts.

|G   **D/F♯**   **|G**   **D**
To - geth - er   for - ev - er.

Chorus

‖**A** |**C♯m** |
Never say goodbye,   never say goodbye.

D |
You and me and my old friends,

Dm |
Hoping it would never end.

A |**C♯m** |
Say goodbye,   never say goodbye.

D |
Holdin' on, we got to try.

Dm |**A** |**C♯m** |**D** |**Dm**   ‖
Holdin' on to never say goodbye.

Verse 2

A |
    Remember days of skipping school,

C♯m
Racing cars, and being cool?

        |**G**
With a six-pack and the radio,

        |**D** |
We   didn't need no place to go.

A |
    Remember at the prom that night,

C♯m
You and me, we had a fight?

        |**G**
But the band, they played our favorite song

        |**D**
And   I held you in my arms so strong.

        |**A**
We danced so close, we danced so slow,

        |**C♯m**
And I swore I'd never let you go.

    |**G**   **D/F♯** |**G**   **D**
To - geth - er   for - ev - er.

Repeat Chorus

Verse 3
     ‖**A**
I guess you'd say we used to talk
      |**C♯m**
About busting out. We'd break their hearts.
    |**G** **D/F♯** |**G** **D**
To - geth - er for - ev - er.

Repeat Chorus

Nights in White Satin

Words and Music by Justin Hayward

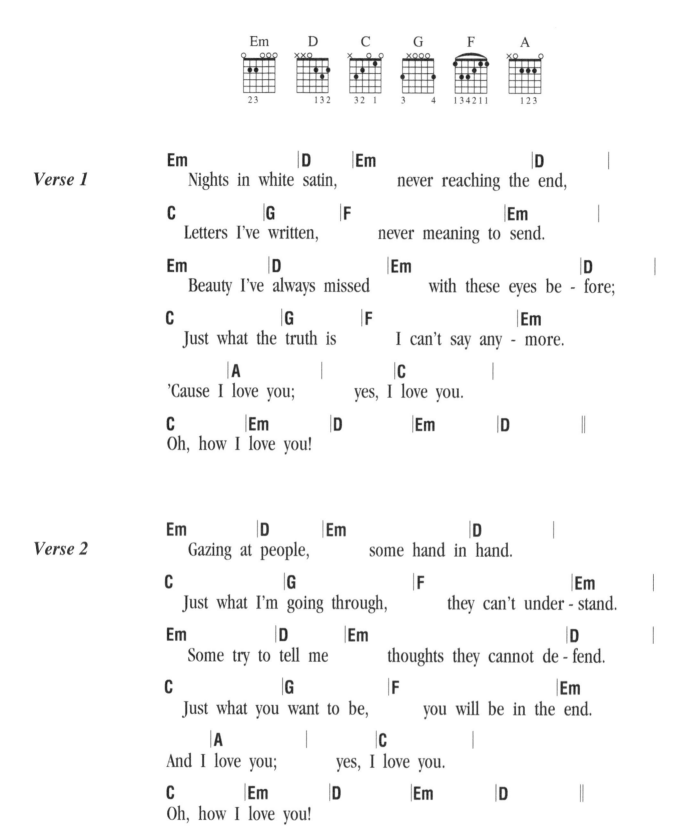

Em   D   C   G   F   A

Verse 1

Em |D |Em |D |
Nights in white satin,   never reaching the end,

C |G |F |Em |
Letters I've written,   never meaning to send.

Em |D |Em |D |
Beauty I've always missed   with these eyes be - fore;

C |G |F |Em |
Just what the truth is   I can't say any - more.

       |A | |C |
'Cause I love you;   yes, I love you.

C |Em |D |Em |D ||
Oh, how I love you!

Verse 2

Em |D |Em |D |
Gazing at people,   some hand in hand.

C |G |F |Em |
Just what I'm going through,   they can't under - stand.

Em |D |Em |D |
Some try to tell me   thoughts they cannot de - fend.

C |G |F |Em |
Just what you want to be,   you will be in the end.

       |A | |C |
And I love you;   yes, I love you.

C |Em |D |Em |D ||
Oh, how I love you!

Repeat Verse 1

Proud Mary

Words and Music by
John Fogerty

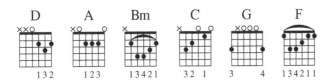

Verse 1

D
Left a good job in the cit - y.

D
Workin' for the man every night and day.

D
And I never lost one min - ute of sleepin'

D
Worryin' 'bout the way things might have been.

A
Big wheel, keep on turn - in'.

Bm
Proud   Mary, keep on burn - in'.

D
Roll - in',   roll - in',

D
Roll - in' on the river.

Verse 2

D
Cleaned a lot of plates in Mem - phis.

D
Pumped a lot of 'pane down in New Orleans.

D
But I never saw the good   side of the city

D
Till I hitched a ride on a riverboat queen.

A
Big wheel, keep on turn - in'.

| **Bm**
Proud   Mary, keep on burn - in'.

| **D**
Roll - in',   roll - in',

| **D**
Roll - in' on the river.

Interlude   C   A | C   A | C   A   G   F | D   F   D |

          D | ||

66

Verse 3

D | |
If you come down to the riv - er,

D | |
Bet you gonna find some peo - ple who live.

D | |
You don't have to worry 'cause you have no money.

D | ||
People on the river are hap - py to give.

A |
Big wheel, keep on turn - in'.

     |**Bm** |
Proud   Mary, keep on burn - in'.

 |**D** |
Roll - in',   roll - in',

 |**D** | ||
Roll - in' on the river.

Outro

 |**D** |
Roll - in',   roll - in',

 |**D** |
Roll - in' on the river.

 |**D** |
Roll - in',   roll - in',

 |**D** | ||
Roll - in' on the river.

Puff the Magic Dragon

Words and Music by
Lenny Lipton and Peter Yarrow

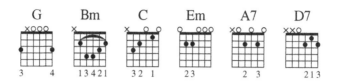

Verse 1

G |**Bm** |**C** |**G**
Puff, the magic dragon lived by the sea

  |**C** |**G**   **Em** |**A7** |**D7** |
And frolicked in the autumn mist in a land called Honah-Lee.

G |**Bm** |**C** |**G**
Little Jackie Paper loved that rascal, Puff,

  |**C** |**G**   **Em** |**A7**   **D7** |**G**   **D7** ||
And brought him strings and sealing wax and other fancy stuff, oh!

Chorus

 G |**Bm** |**C** |**G**
Puff, the magic dragon lived by the sea

  |**C** |**G**   **Em** |**A7** |**D7** |
And frolicked in the autumn mist in a land called Honah-Lee.

G |**Bm** |**C** |**G**
Puff, the magic dragon lived by the sea

  |**C** |**G**   **Em** |**A7**   **D7** |**G**
And frolicked in the autumn mist in a land called Honah-Lee.

Verse 2

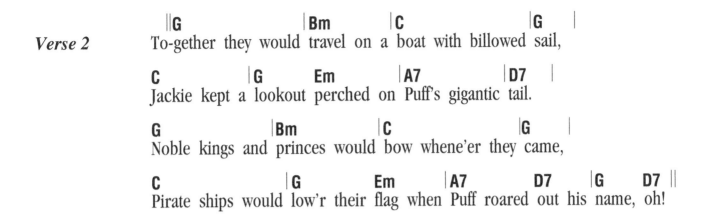

```
  ||G                    |Bm        |C                  |G        |
    To-gether they would travel on a boat with billowed sail,

  C          |G   Em      |A7          |D7       |
    Jackie kept a lookout perched on Puff's gigantic tail.

  G                  |Bm        |C                  |G        |
    Noble kings and princes would bow whene'er they came,

  C                    |G   Em      |A7        D7   |G    D7 ||
    Pirate ships would low'r their flag when Puff roared out his name, oh!
```

Repeat Chorus

Verse 3

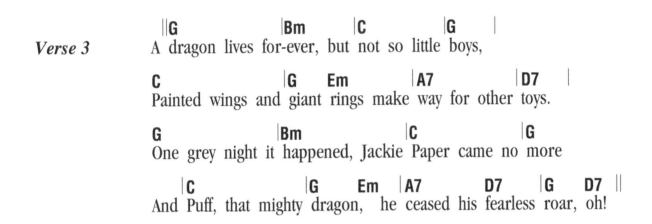

```
    ||G              |Bm      |C              |G        |
      A dragon lives for-ever, but not so little boys,

  C                  |G   Em      |A7          |D7       |
    Painted wings and giant rings make way for other toys.

  G                    |Bm            |C                |G
    One grey night it happened, Jackie Paper came no more

     |C                  |G   Em    |A7        D7   |G    D7 ||
      And Puff, that mighty dragon,  he ceased his fearless roar, oh!
```

Repeat Chorus

Verse 4

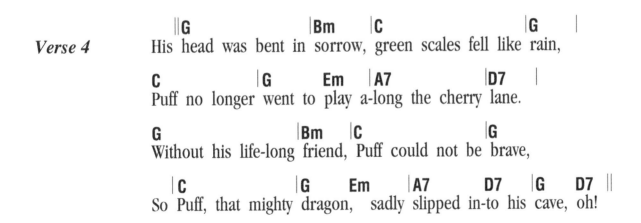

```
    ||G              |Bm    |C                  |G        |
      His head was bent in sorrow, green scales fell like rain,

  C              |G   Em    |A7          |D7       |
    Puff no longer went to play a-long the cherry lane.

  G                  |Bm    |C                |G
    Without his life-long friend, Puff could not be brave,

     |C                  |G   Em    |A7        D7   |G    D7 ||
      So Puff, that mighty dragon,  sadly slipped in-to his cave, oh!
```

Repeat Chorus

Realize

Words and Music by
Colbie Caillat, Jason Reeves and Mikal Blue

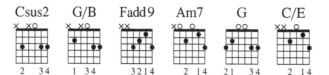

Verse 1

Csus2
   Take time to realize
G/B
   That your warmth is
Fadd9   **Am7** |**G/B**
Crashing down   on in.
Csus2
   Take time to realize
G/B
   That I am on your side.
Fadd9   **Am7** |**G/B**
   Didn't I, didn't I tell you?

Pre-Chorus

Fadd9   **Am7**
   But I can't spell it out for you.
G
   No, it's never gonna be that simple.
Fadd9   **Am7** |**G/B**
   No, I can't spell it out for you.

Chorus 1

‖**Csus2**　　　　　　　**G/B**
If you just realize what I just realized,
　　　　　　|**Am7**　　　　　　　　　　**Fadd9**
Then we'd be perfect for each other and we'll never find another.
　　|**Csus2**　　　　　**G/B**
Just realize what I just realized.
　　　|**Am7**　　　　　　**Fadd9**　　　　　　　　　　|
We'd never have to wonder if we missed out on each other now.
Csus2　　　　**G/B**　　　|**Am7**　　　**Fadd9**　　　‖

Verse 2

Csus2　　　　　　　　　　　　|
　　　Take time to realize,
G/B　　　　　　　　　　|
　　Oh, oh, I'm on your side.
Fadd9　　　**Am7**　　　　|**G**　　　|
　　　Didn't I,　　didn't I tell　you?
Csus2　　　　　　　　|
　　Take time to realize
G/B　　　　　　　　　　　　|**Fadd9**　　**Am7**
　　This all can pass you by.
　　　　　　|**G/B**　　　‖
Didn't I tell　you?

Repeat Pre-Chorus

Chorus 2

‖**Csus2**　　　　　　　**G/B**
If you just realize what I just realized,
　　　　　　|**Am7**　　　　　　　　　　**Fadd9**
Then we'd be perfect for each other and we'll never find another.
　　|**Csus2**　　　　　**G/B**
Just realize what I just realized.
　　|**Am7**　　　　　　**Fadd9**　　　　　　　　　‖
We'd never have to wonder if we missed out on each other but...

Bridge

```
Am7                   G/B        |
     It's not the same,
Fadd9                            G
       No, it's never the same
  |Am7 G/B    Csus2 C/E|F           |
If you  don't  feel   it    too.
Am7                              G          |
     If you meet me halfway,
Fadd9                              G
       If you would  meet  me  half - way,
          |Am7  G/B  Csus2  C/E      |Fadd9
It  could  be     the   same  for  you.
```

Chorus 3

```
          ||Csus2                 G/B
If you just realize what I just realized,
                |Am7                        Fadd9
Then we'd be perfect for each other and we'll never find another.
     |Csus2            G/B
Just realize what I just realized.
     |Am7                  Fadd9
We'd never have to wonder.
     |Csus2                G/B         |Am7          Fadd9
Just realize what I just realized.
          |Csus2               G/B        |Am7          Fadd9
If you just realize what I just realized…
```

Outro

```
     |Csus2        G/B          |Am7
Oo,         oo.
Fadd9                              |Csus2
Missed out on each other now,
   G/B                               |Am7        Fadd9 |
We missed out on each other now,      ow, ow,       yeah.
Csus2   G/B       |Am7       Fadd9     |Csus2       G/B
    Real - ize,  real - ize,  real - ize,  real - ize,
       |Am7    Fadd9 |Csus2          |G/B          |Fadd9  Am7    |G/B        ||
Oo, oo.
```

Rocky Mountain High

Words and Music by
John Denver and Mike Taylor

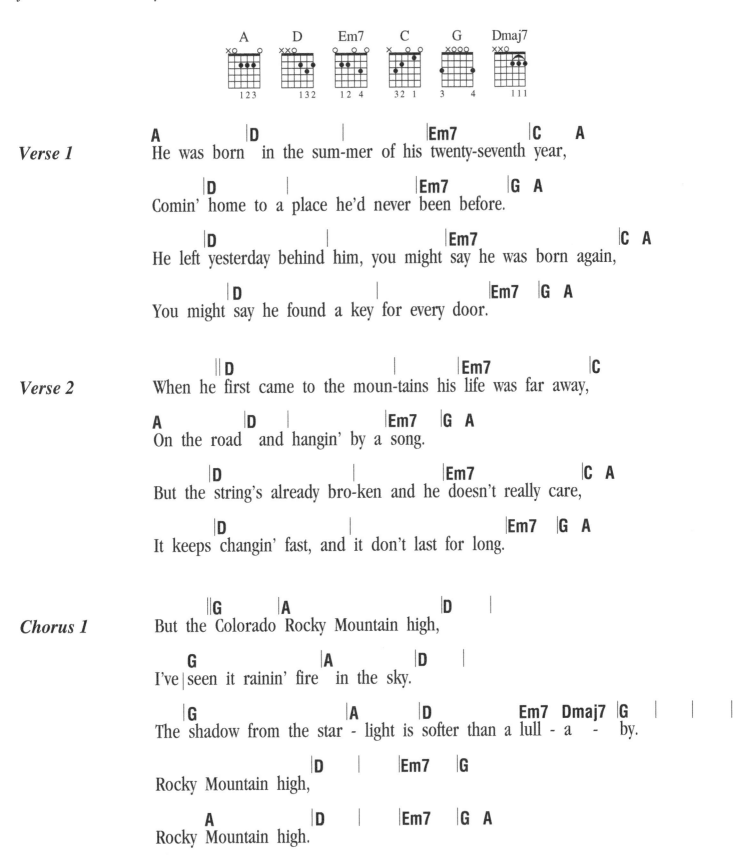

Verse 1

A | D | | Em7 | C A
He was born in the sum-mer of his twenty-seventh year,

| D | | Em7 | G A
Comin' home to a place he'd never been before.

| D | | Em7 | C A
He left yesterday behind him, you might say he was born again,

| D | | Em7 | G A
You might say he found a key for every door.

Verse 2

|| D | | Em7 | C
When he first came to the moun-tains his life was far away,

A | D | | Em7 | G A
On the road and hangin' by a song.

| D | | Em7 | C A
But the string's already bro-ken and he doesn't really care,

| D | | Em7 | G A
It keeps changin' fast, and it don't last for long.

Chorus 1

|| G | A | D | |
But the Colorado Rocky Mountain high,

G | A | D | |
I've | seen it rainin' fire in the sky.

| G | A | D | Em7 Dmaj7 | G | | |
The shadow from the star - light is softer than a lull - a - by.

| D | | Em7 | G
Rocky Mountain high,

A | D | | Em7 | G A
Rocky Mountain high.

Verse 3

‖**D** | |**Em7** |**C A**
He climbed Cathedral Moun-tains, he saw silver clouds below,

|**D** | |**Em7** |**G A**
He saw everything as far as you can see.

|**D** | |**Em7** |**C A**
And they say that he got cra-zy once and he tried to touch the sun,

|**D** | |**Em7** |**G A**
And he lost a friend but kept his memory.

Verse 4

‖**D** | |**Em7** |**C**
Now he walks in quiet sol-itude the forests and the streams,

A |**D** | |**Em7** |**G A**
Seeking grace in every step he takes.

|**D** | |**Em7** |**C A**
His sight has turned inside himself to try and understand

|**D** | |**Em7** |**G A**
The se-renity of a clear blue mountain lake.

Chorus 2

‖**G** |**A** |**D** |
And the Colorado Rocky Mountain high,

|**G** |**A** |**D** | |**G**
I've seen it rainin' fire in the sky.

|**A** |**D Em7 Dmaj7** |**G** | | |
Talk to God and listen to the cas-ual re - ply.

|**D** | |**Em7** |**G**
Rocky Mountain high,

A |**D** | |**Em7** |**G A**
Rocky Mountain high.

Verse 5

‖D | |Em7 |C   A
Now his life is full of won-der but his heart still knows some fear

|D | |Em7 |G A
Of a simple thing he cannot compre-hend:

|D | |Em7 |C   A
Why they try to tear the moun-tains down to bring in a couple more

|D | |Em7 |G A
More people, more scars upon the land.

Chorus 3

‖G |A   D |
And the Colorado Rocky Mountain high,

|G |A |D |
I've seen it rainin' fire in the sky.

|G |A |D   Em7 Dmaj7 |G | | |
I know he'd be a poor - er man if he never saw an ea - gle   fly.

|D | |Em7 |G
Rocky Mountain high,

A |D |
Rocky Mountain high.

Outro-Chorus

‖G |A |D |
It's a Colorado Rock - y Mountain high,

|G |A |D | |
I've seen it rainin' fire in the sky.

G |A |D   Em7 D |G | | |
Friends around the camp - fire and everybod - y's high.

|D | |Em7 |G
Rocky Mountain high,

A |D | |Em7 |G
Rocky Mountain high,

A |D | |Em7 |G
Rocky Mountain high,

A |D | ‖
Rocky Mountain high.

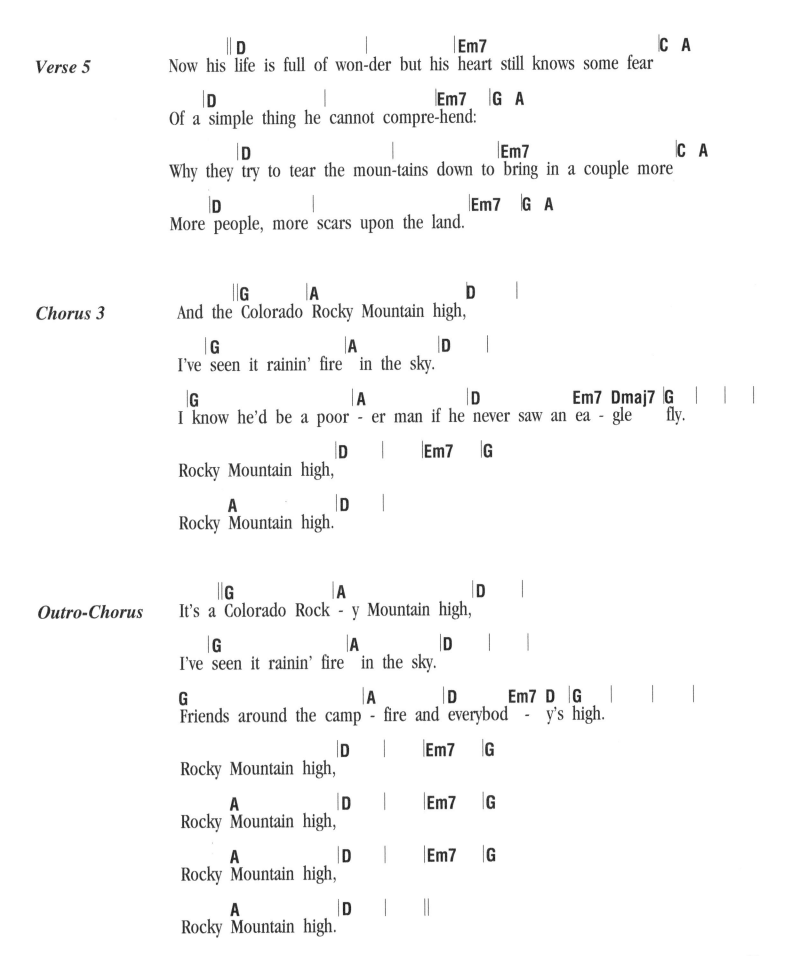

Redemption Song

Words and Music by
Bob Marley

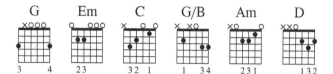

Verse 1

|G |Em
Old pirates, yes, they rob I,

    |C   G/B |Am |
Sold I to the merchant ships

G |Em |
Minutes after they took I

C   G/B |Am
From the bottomless pit.

    |G |Em |
But my hand was made strong

C   G/B |Am
By the hand of the Al - mighty.

    |G |Em
We forward in this gener - ation

C |D |
Triumphant - ly.

Chorus

    D   ‖G |
Won't you help to sing

    C   D |G
These songs of freedom?

       |C   D |Em |
'Cause all I ever have,

    C   D |G |
Re - demption songs,

    C   D |G |C   D
Re - demption songs.

Verse 2

        ‖G |Em
Emanci - pate yourselves from mental slavery.

       |C   G/B |Am
None but our - selves can free our minds.

    |G |Em
Have no fear for atomic energy,

      |C   G/B |D
'Cause none of them can stop the time.

   |G |Em
How long shall they kill our prophets

    |C   G/B |Am
While we stand a - side and look? Ooh.

   |G |Em
Some say it's just a part of it;

  |C   G/B |D |
We've got to ful - fill the book.

Repeat Chorus

Repeat Verse 2

Repeat Chorus

Satellite

Music by Miller, Gardner, Rosenworcel and Pisapia
Words by Rosenworcel, Miller and Pisapia

(Capo 2nd fret)

Em   C   Am   D   G

Intro   **Em** | **|C** **|Am** |

              Em | **|C** **|Am** |

              Am | | |

Verse 1

          ||Em **|D** **|Am** |
Shining like a work of art.

          |Em **|D** **|Am** |
Hanging on a wall of stars.

          |Em **|D** **|C** | **|Am** | **||**
Are you what I think you are?

Chorus

Em **|G** **|C** | |
You're my satellite.

Em **|G** **|C** |
You're riding with me tonight.

         |Em **|G**
Passenger side, lighting the sky,

         |C **|Am** |
Always the first star that I find.

Em **|G** **|C** | **||**
You're my satellite.

Interlude 1   **Em** | **|C** **|Am** | |

Verse 2

‖Em |D |Am |
Elevator to   the moon,

|Em |D |Am |
Whistling a fa - vorite tune.

|Em |D |C | |Am | ‖
Trying to get a clos - er view.

Repeat Chorus

Interlude 2

Em | |C |Am |

Em | |C |Am |

Am | | |

Verse 3

‖Em |D |Am |
Maybe you will al - ways be

|Em |D |C | |Am | ‖
Just a little out of reach.

Interlude 3

Em |G |C | |

Em |G |C | |

Em |G |C |Am |

Em |G |C | ‖

Repeat Chorus

Em |G |C | ‖
You're my satellite.

Outro

Em |G |C | |

Em |G |C |Am |Em   ‖

Sleep All Day

Words and Music by
Jason Mraz

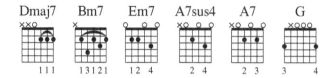

Intro

Dmaj7 | Bm7 | Em7 | A7sus4 A7 |
Scat sing...
Dmaj7 | Bm7 | Em7 | A7sus4 A7

Verse 1

          ‖Dmaj7 |Bm7
Well, his after moan though cries, "Oh,   no."
       |Em7 |A7sus4   A7
He's building up a shine, but he take it   slow.
            |Dmaj7 |Bm7
And he knows it's time to make a change   here,
     |Em7 |A7sus4   A7
And time to get away.
          |Dmaj7 |Bm7
And he knows it's   time for all the wrong reasons,
   |Em7 |A7sus4   A7
Oh, time to end the pain.

Chorus 1

          ‖Dmaj7 |
But he   sleep all, we sleep all day,
Bm7 |Em7 |A7sus4   A7
    Sleep all, we sleep all day   over.
         |Dmaj7 |
Why don't we,   sleep all, we sleep all day?
Bm7 |Em7 |A7sus4   A7
    Sleep all, we sleep all day   over.

Verse 2

‖Dmaj7

She said, uh,　　　"What would your mother think of all this?

Bm7

　　How would your father react?

|Em7　　　　　　　　　　　　　　　　　　　|A7sus4　　A7

Oh,　　would he take it all back, what they've　　done?"

"No way," they said.

Dmaj7

　　Take it, take it." "He said,

Bm7　　　　　　　　|Em7

　　Make it with your own　　two　hands."

A7sus4　　　　　A7

　　That was my old man, and he said,

|Em7

"If　　all is grounded, you should

G　　　　　　　　　　　|Dmaj7

　Go make a mountain out of it,　　it."

Verse 3

‖Dmaj7　　　　　　　　　　|Bm7

Oh, what a lovely day to have slice of humble pie.

|Em7　　　　　　　　　　　|A7sus4　　A7

Oh, re - calling of the while we used to drive and drive

|Dmaj7　　|Bm7　　　　|Em7

Here and there,　　going no - where　but　for us.

|A7sus4　　　　A7

Nowhere but the　　two of us.

|Dmaj7　　　　　　　|Bm7

And we knew it was　　time to take a chance　here,

|Em7　　　　　　|A7sus4　　　　A7

And time to compromise our lives just　　a little while.

|Dmaj7　　　　　　　|Bm7

And it was time for all the wrong and lone - ly, lonesome reasons.

|Em7　　　　　|A7sus4　　A7

But time　is often on my side, but I give it to you　tonight.

Chorus 2

‖**Dmaj7** |

And we   sleep all, we sleep all day,

Bm7   **|Em7**   **|A7sus4**   **A7**

Sleep all, we sleep all day   over.

|Dmaj7

Why don't we,   sleep all, we sleep all day?

Bm7   **|Em7**   **|A7sus4 A7**

We sleep all, we sleep all day o - ver, and over, over and over a - gain.

Verse 4

‖**Dmaj7** |

And, as the time   goes by, we get a little bit tired,

Bm7   **|Em7**   **|A7sus4**   **A7**

Waking and baked another Marlboro mile   wide.

|Dmaj7   **|Bm7**

It's sending the boys   on the run in the time in the hot summer sun

|Em7

To swim beneath, over, out - side.

|A7sus4   **A7**

Still they're reading between the lines.

|Dmaj7

But they re - member the part in the Hallmark card,

|Bm7 |

Where they read about the dreams, and they're reaching for the stars

Em7   **|A7sus4**   **A7**

To hold on a little bit closer to.

|Dmaj7 |

Oo, they knew it was time, time to take, a take love,

Bm7 |

Time to take a chance here,

Em7   **|A7sus4**   **A7**

Time to compromise, to occu - py the lives.

|Dmaj7   **|Bm7**

And then there was time for all the wrong rea - sons, oh.

|Em7   **|A7sus4**   **A7**   ‖

But, oh, time   is often on my side, but I give it to you. Oh, boy.

Chorus 3

Dmaj7
    Sleep all, we sleep all day,

Bm7   **Em7**
  Sleep all, we sleep all day   over.

     A7sus4   **A7**
La - din   - din - din - da, okay.

                 Dmaj7
So, why don't we,   sleep all, we sleep all day?

Bm7   **Em7**   **A7sus4**   **A7**
  Sleep all, we sleep all day   over   and over.

Verse 5

    Dmaj7
She said, "What would your mother think of all this?

Bm7
  How would your father react? Oh, Lord.

Em7   **A7sus4**   **A7**
  Would he take it all back, what they've done?"

       Dmaj7
"No way," they said. "Take it, take it, take it," he said.

Bm7   **Em7**
"Make it, don't break it with your own   two hands."

     A7sus4   **A7**
Said that   was my old man, and he said,

    Em7   **G**   **Dmaj7**
"If all,   all is grounded, you should   go make a mountain out of it.

Outro

                                   |Bm7   **|Em7**
Lord, go make a mountain out of it, go   on and on and on   and on.

            |A7sus4   **A7**   **|Dmaj7**   **|Bm7**
Well, you should go   on, make a mountain out of   it.

     |Em7   **|A7sus4**   **A7**
Hey, love. Go on, go   on and go on

    |Dmaj7   **|**
And go on and make a mountain.

Bm7   **|Em7**
   Go on and make a mountain, go   on.

        |A7sus4   **A7**   **|Dmaj7** **|**   **||**
You should go   on and make a mountain out of it.

Taylor

Words and Music by Jack Johnson

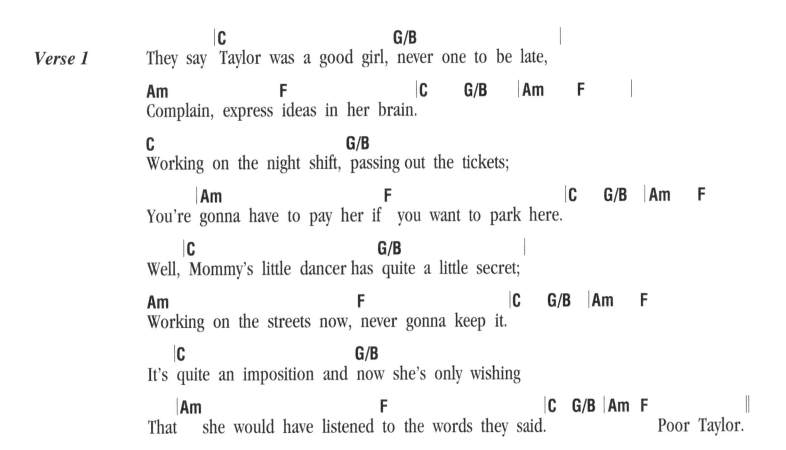

Verse 1

|C   G/B |
They say Taylor was a good girl, never one to be late,

Am   **F** |**C**   **G/B** |**Am**   **F** |
Complain, express ideas in her brain.

C   **G/B**
Working on the night shift, passing out the tickets;

    |**Am**   **F** |**C**   **G/B** |**Am**   **F**
You're gonna have to pay her if you want to park here.

     |**C**   **G/B** |
Well, Mommy's little dancer has quite a little secret;

Am   **F** |**C**   **G/B** |**Am**   **F**
Working on the streets now, never gonna keep it.

    |**C**   **G/B**
It's quite an imposition and now she's only wishing

 |**Am**   **F** |**C** **G/B** |**Am** **F**   ‖
That   she would have listened to the words they said.   Poor Taylor.

Chorus

```
     C          G            |Am        F              |
      She just wanders around,      unaf - fected by

     C       G              |Am     F                 |
       The winter winds, yeah,    and she'll pretend that

     C       G              |Am    F                 |
       She's somewhere else     so far and clear,

     C       G              |Am                    ||
       About two thousand miles        from here.
```

Interlude

```
     C     G/B   |Am    F    |C     G/B   |Am    F       ||
```

Verse 2

```
     C              G/B               |Am         F
     Peter Patrick pit - ter patters on the win - dow,

      |C             G/B              |Am     F    |
     But Sunny Silhouette     won't let him     in.

     C              G/B                  |Am        F
     Poor old Pete's got nothing 'cause he's been falling;

       |C             G/B              |Am      F
     Somehow Sunny knows   just where he's     been.

                      |C                       G/B        |Am     F    |
     He thinks that sing - ing on Sunday's gonna save his soul,

     C     G/B   |Am        F      |
     Now that Saturday's     gone.

     C              G/B             |Am          F
     Sometimes he thinks    that he's on    his way,

                    |C     G/B   |Am
     But I could see

              F                    ||
     That his brake lights are on.
```

Chorus
```
        C          G        |Am       F             |
        He just wanders around,    unaf - fected by

        C      G           |Am     F               |
        The winter winds, yeah,    and he'll pretend that

        C      G             |Am  F               |
        He's somewhere else    so far and clear,

        C         G              |Am                ‖
        About two thousand miles      from here.
```

Interlude
```
        C     G/B   |Am    F    |C     G/B   |Am    F
```

Verse 3
```
                      ‖C              G/B
        She's such a tough   enchilada filled   up with nada,

        |Am                        F              |C     G/B   |Am      F
        Giv - ing what she gotta give  to get a dollar bill.

               |C                 G/B
        Used to be   a limber chicken; time's    a been a ticking.

           |Am                F
        Now    she's finger licking to the man

              |C                 G/B
        With the money in his pocket, fly - ing in his rocket,

          |Am                     F               |
        On - ly stopping by on his way to a better world.

        C   D  |F   G                     |
                  If Taylor finds a better world,

        C   D  |F     G                        |C       |Fmaj7   ‖
                  Then Taylor's gonna run away.
```

Take Me Home, Country Roads

Words and Music by
John Denver, Bill Danoff and Taffy Nivert

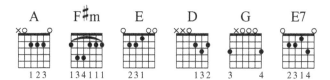

Verse 1

A | | F♯m | |E
Almost heaven,   West Virgin-ia,

|E | D |A | |
Blue Ridge Mountains, Shenandoah River.

A | | F♯m | |
Life is old there, older than the trees,

E | |D |A
Younger than the mountains, growin' like a breeze.

Chorus

‖A | |E |
Country roads, take me home

|F♯m | |D |
To the place I be-long:

|A | |E |
West Vir-ginia, mountain momma,

|D | |A | ‖
Take me home, country roads.

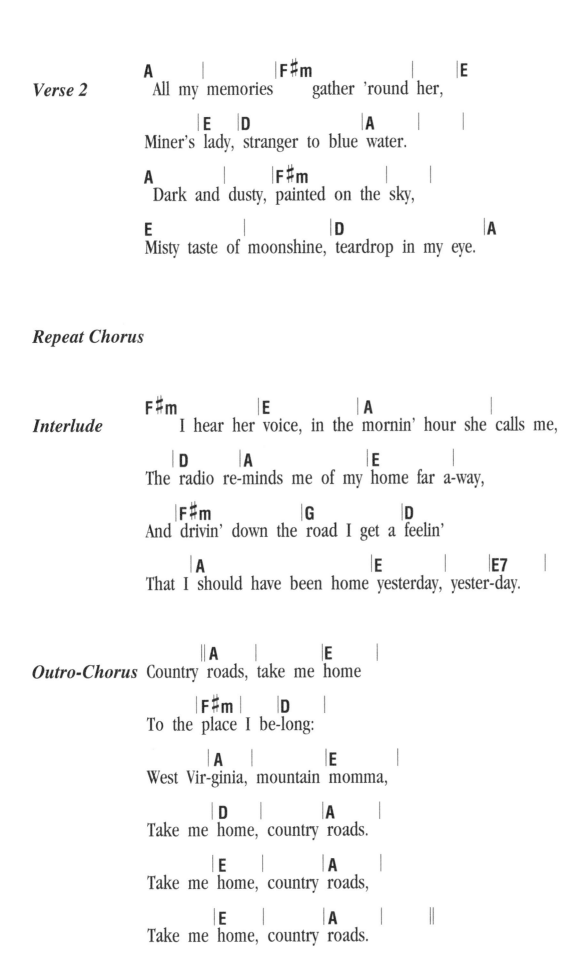

Verse 2

    A | **|F♯m** | **|E**
All my memories   gather 'round her,

    |E   **|D**   **|A** | |
Miner's lady, stranger to blue water.

A | **|F♯m** | |
 Dark and dusty, painted on the sky,

E | **|D**   **|A**
Misty taste of moonshine, teardrop in my eye.

Repeat Chorus

Interlude

F♯m   **|E**   **|A** |
      I hear her voice, in the mornin' hour she calls me,

 |D   **|A**   **|E** |
The radio re-minds me of my home far a-way,

 |F♯m   **|G**   **|D**
And drivin' down the road I get a feelin'

 |A   **|E** | **|E7** |
That I should have been home yesterday, yester-day.

Outro-Chorus

    ||A | **|E** |
Country roads, take me home

   |F♯m| **|D** |
To the place I be-long:

    |A | **|E** |
West Vir-ginia, mountain momma,

    |D | **|A** |
Take me home, country roads.

    |E | **|A** |
Take me home, country roads,

    |E | **|A** | ||
Take me home, country roads.

Tell Her
(Tell Him)

Words and Music by
Bert Russell

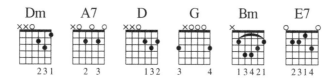

Verse 1

Dm |**A7** |**Dm**
I know something about love, you gotta want it bad.

                   |**A7** |
If that guy's got into your blood, go out and get him.

D |**G** |**D**
If you want him to be   the very part of you,

                      |**A7** ||
Makes you want to breathe,   here's the thing to do:

Chorus

D |
Tell him that you're never gonna leave him.

G |
Tell him that you're always gonna love him.

D   **A7** |**Dm** ||
Tell him, tell him, tell him, tell him right now.

Verse 2

Dm |**A7** |
I   know something about love, you gotta show it

Dm |**A7** |
And make him see the moon up a-bove, reach out and get it.

D |**G** |**D**
If you want him,   makes your heart sing out,

                |**A7** ||
If you want him to   only think of you:

Repeat Chorus

Bridge

   ‖D |Bm
Ever since the world began,   it's been that way for man.

 |G |A7 |D |
And women were cre-ated to make love their destiny.

G |E7 |A7
 Then why should true love be so compli-cated?

          ‖
Oh yeah, uh-huh!

Verse 3

Dm |A7 |
  I know something about love, gotta take it

Dm |A7 |
And show him what the world's made of, one kiss will prove it.

D |G |D
 If you want him to be always by your side,

          |A7   ‖
Take his hand tonight, swallow your foolish pride.

Outro-Chorus

D |
Tell him that you're never gonna leave him.

G |
Tell him that you're always gonna love him.

D   A7 |D |
Tell him, tell him, tell him, tell him right now.

D |
Tell him that you're never gonna leave him.

G |
Tell him that you're always gonna love him.

D   A7 |D   ‖
Tell him, tell him, tell him, tell him right now.

Tripping Billies

Words and Music by
David J. Matthews

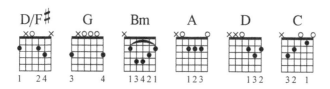

D/F# G Bm A D C

Intro

D/F# G | D/F# G | Bm A D/F# G | |D/F# G A Bm   D/F# G|

G   D/F# G | Bm A D/F# G | |D/F# G A Bm ||

Verse 1

    A   D
    We were a - bove;
C | Bm
You were standing un - derneath us.
    |A   D | D/F#   G |
We were not   yet lo - vers.
A   D
    Dragons were smoked,
C | Bm
Bum - blebees were sting - ing us.
     |A   D | D/F#   G
I was   soon   to be cra - zy.

Chorus 1

          ||Bm   A |D/F#   G   A   Bm
Eat, drink,   and be   merry,
A |Bm   A |D/F#   G   A   Bm
For to - morrow we   die.
        |Bm   A |D/F#   G   A   Bm
Eat, drink,   and be   merry,
A |Bm   A |D/F#   G   A   Bm
For to - morrow we   die.
            |A   D   C|
'Cause we're tripping billies.
C   Bm |A   D | D/F# G |A   D   C|

C   Bm |A   D | D/F# G ||

Verse 2

```
     A                D
     We're wearing nothing,
C    |                   Bm
Noth - ing but our shad - ows.
          |A        D              | D/F♯  G        |
Shadows      falling down on the beach   sand.
A                D
     Remembering once,
C    |               Bm
Out on the beach - es.
          |A         D            | D/F♯  G
We wore    pineapple    grass brace - lets.
```

Chorus 2

```
        ‖Bm        A         |D/F♯   G   A   Bm
So why      would you care
A    |Bm        A         |D/F♯   G   A   Bm
To get out of this    place?
          |Bm         A         |D/F♯   G   A   Bm
You and me    and all    our friends,
A    |Bm        A            |D/F♯  G   A   Bm  D/F♯  G |
Such a happy hu - man race,           yeah!
G      D/F♯   G|  Bm  A  D/F♯  G|            |D/F♯  G  A  Bm  D/F♯  G |

G      D/F♯   G|  Bm  A  D/F♯  G|            |D/F♯  G  A  Bm

          |A        D         C|
'Cause we're tripping billies.
C    Bm    |A    D      | D/F♯ G    |A    D    C|

C    Bm    |A    D      | D/F♯ G        ‖
```
```
```

Verse 3

```
        A            D
    We are all sitting,
    C  |            Bm          |
    Legs   crossed, 'round    a fire.
    A          D              | D/F♯  G        |
    My yellow   flame, she danc - es.
    A          D
    Tequila drinking,
    C  |          Bm              |
    Oh,   our minds    will wander
    A      D          | D/F♯  G
    To    wondrous plac - es.
```

Chorus 3

```
            ‖ Bm        A        | D/F♯  G  A  Bm
    So why      would you care
    A    | Bm        A        | D/F♯  G  A  Bm
    To get out of this    place?
               | Bm        A        | D/F♯  G  A  Bm
    You and me     and all    our friends,
    A    | Bm        A        | D/F♯  G  A  Bm
    Such a happy hu - man race.
               | Bm        A        | D/F♯  G  A  Bm
    Eat, drink,    and be    merry,
    A    | Bm        A        | D/F♯  G  A  Bm
    For to - morrow we   die.
               | Bm        A        | D/F♯  G  A  Bm
    Eat, drink,    and be    merry,
    A    | Bm        A        |
    For to - morrow we   die.
    D/F♯ G      A     Bm                 ‖
        Take it, moun - tain boy.
```

Interlude

```
    Bm      A        | D/F♯ G A Bm A | Bm        A          | D/F♯ G A Bm        |

    Bm      A        | D/F♯ G A Bm A | Bm        A          | D/F♯ G A  Bm
```

94

Chorus 4

```
               ‖Bm       A              |D/F♯ G  A  Bm
Eat,  drink,       and  be  merry,
A     |Bm       A              |D/F♯ G  A  Bm
For  to - morrow  we  die.
               |Bm       A              |D/F♯ G  A  Bm
Eat,  drink,       and  be  merry,
A     |Bm       A              |D/F♯ G  A  Bm
For  to - morrow  we  die.
               |Bm       A              |D/F♯ G  A  Bm
Eat,  drink,       and  be  merry,
A     |Bm       A              |D/F♯ G  A  Bm
For  to - morrow  we  die.
               |Bm       A              |D/F♯ G  A  Bm
Eat,  drink,       and  be  merry,
A     |Bm       A              |D/F♯ G  A  Bm      D/F♯  G ‖
For  to - morrow  we  die.                 Yeah!
```

Outro

```
G      D/F♯   G |  Bm  A  D/F♯  G |          |D/F♯ G  A  Bm   D/F♯ G |

G      D/F♯   G |  Bm  A  D/F♯  G |          |D/F♯ G  A  Bm  |             ‖
```

Waiting on the World to Change

Words and Music by
John Mayer

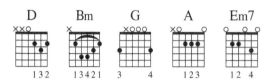

Intro   D   Bm |G   D |A   Bm |G   D   ‖

Verse 1

D   Bm |G   D
   Me and all my friends, we're all   misunder - stood.

|A   Bm |G   D
They say we stand for nothing and there's no way we ever could.

|D   Bm
Now we see   everything that's going wrong

|G   D
With the world and those who lead it.

|A   Bm |G   D
We just feel like we don't   have the means to rise above and beat it.

Chorus 1

‖D   Bm |G   D
So we keep waiting (waiting), waiting on the world to change.

|A   Bm |G   D
We keep on waiting (waiting), waiting on the world to change.

|D   Em7 |Bm   Em7
It's hard to beat the system when we're standing at a distance.

|A   Bm |G   D
So we keep waiting (waiting), waiting on the world to change.

Verse 2

```
   ‖D              Bm                    |G           D
Now, if we had the power to bring our neigh-bors home from war,
          |A          Bm              |G           D
They would have never missed a Christmas; no more ribbons on their door.
          |D          Bm          |G           D
And when you trust your tele-vision, what you get is what you got.
          |A          Bm              |G           D
'Cause when they own the infor - mation, oh, they can bend it all they want.
```

Chorus 2

```
                    ‖D  Bm                 |G           D
That's why we're wait - ing (waiting), waiting on the world to change.
          |A      Bm              |G           D
We keep on waiting (waiting), waiting on the world to change.
   |D              Em7         |Bm              Em7
It's not that we don't care; we just know     that the fight ain't    fair.
          |A      Bm              |G           D
So we keep on waiting (waiting), waiting on the world to change.
```

Chorus 3

```
          ‖D          Bm                 |G           D
And we're still waiting (waiting), waiting on the world to change.
          |A      Bm              |G           D
We keep on waiting (waiting), waiting on the world to change.
   |D              Em7         |Bm              Em7
One day our gener - ation is gonna rule the popu - lation.
          |A      Bm              |G           D
So we keep on waiting (waiting), waiting on the world to change.
```

Outro

          ‖**A**   **Bm** |**G**   **D**
I know we keep on waiting (waiting), waiting on the world to change.

       |**A**   **Bm** |**G**   **D**
We keep on waiting (waiting), we're waiting on the world to change.

       |**G**   **D**
Waiting on the world to change.

       |**G**   **D**
Waiting on the world to change.

       |**G**   **D**   ‖
Waiting on the world to change.

What Would You Say

Words and Music by
David J. Matthews

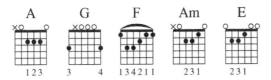

Verse 1

A
  Up and down the puppies' hair,
G |**A**
  Fleas and ticks jump ev - 'rywhere.
            |**G**
'Cause of orig - inal sin.
A
  Down the hill fell Jack and Jill,
  |**G** |**A**
And you came tumbling af - ter.
       |**G** ||
'Cause of orig - inal sin.

Pre-Chorus 1

F |**G**
Rip away the tears,
Am |**G**
Drink a hope to happy years
  |**F**   **E** |**F**   **G** |**A**
And you may find a life - time's passed you by.

Chorus

```
       G                    ‖A
         What would you say?
                        |G
Don't drop the big   one.
                             |A
If you a monkey on a string,
                        |G
Well, don't cut my life - line.
                        |A
If you a doggie on a chain,
                           |G
Well, don't bite the mail - man.
                        |A              |G              ‖
What would you say?
```

Verse 2

```
     A                              |G
       I was there when the bear ate his head;
                          |A
Thought it was a can - dy.
                  |G                  |
Everyone goes     in the end.
     A
       Knock, knock, on the door.
           |G                        |A
Who's    it for? There's nobody in    here.
                    |G
Look in the mir - ror, my friend.
```

Pre-Chorus 2

```
     ‖F                |G
I don't understand at best,
         |Am              |G
And cannot speak for all the rest.
       |F      E      |F      G          |A              |
The morning rise, a life - time's passed me by.
```

Repeat Chorus

Verse 3

```
              A
              Every dog has its day,
                 |G                           |A
              Every day has its way of being for - gotten.
                              |G
              Mom, it's my birthday.
                              |A                          |
              Would you say,    hey? Now, what could you say?
              G                        |A          |G            ||
              What would you say?
```

Repeat Verse 2

Repeat Pre-Chorus 2

Outro

```
              G  N.C.                    |              ||
              What would you say?
```

Who'll Stop the Rain

Words and Music by
John Fogerty

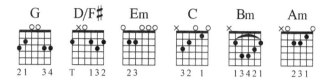

Intro   G | D/F♯ | Em | D/F♯ | G | ‖

Verse 1

G |
Long as I remem - ber,

   | C | G |
The rain been coming down,

G |
Clouds of mystery pour - ing

   | C | G |
Con - fusion on the ground.

C | G |
Good men through the ag - es

C | G |
Trying to find the sun;

C | D |
And I wonder, still I wonder,

Em | G | ‖
Who'll stop the rain?

Verse 2

```
G                    |
I went down Virgin - ia,
      |C                    |G        |
Seeking shelter from the storm.
G              |Bm
Caught up in the fa - ble,
 |C                  |G        |
I watched the tower grow.
C                |G        |
Five-year plans and new   deals
C                |G        |
Wrapped in golden chains.
C          |D        |
And I wonder, still I wonder,
Em              |G        |        ||
Who'll stop the rain?
```

Interlude   C   G   D | |Am   C   Em | D |G | ||

Verse 3

```
G                |        |
Heard the singers play - ing,
C                    |G
How we cheered for more.
   |G                |Bm        |
The crowd had rushed togeth - er,
C                |G        |
Trying to keep warm.
C                |G        |
Still the rain kept pour - ing,
C                |G        |
Falling on my ears.
C          |D        |
And I wonder, still I wonder,
Em              |        ||
Who'll stop the rain?
```

Repeat and fade

Outro ||: G | D/F♯ |Em | D/F♯ :||

You've Got to Hide Your Love Away

Words and Music by
John Lennon and Paul McCartney

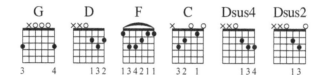

Verse 1

```
G        D      |F    G    |
Here I stand, head in hand,
C                |F    C    |
Turn my face to the wall.
G        D     |F      G       |
If she's gone I can't go on,
C              |F    C    |D         ||
Feeling two foot small.
```

Verse 2

```
G      D    |F    G    |
Every - where people stare,
C          |F    C    |
Each and every day.
G      D     |F      G      |
I can see them laugh at me,
C              |F    C    |D        |          ||
And I hear them say:
```

Chorus

```
G                    |C              |Dsus4   D     |Dsus2   D      |
"Hey, you've got to hide your love a - way!"
G                    |C              |Dsus4   D     |Dsus2   D      ||
"Hey, you've got to hide your love a - way!"
```

Verse 3

```
        G        D  |F    G         |
How can I   even   try?
C              |F   C      |
I  can  never  win.
G        D    |F    G         |
Hearing  them,  seeing  them
C              |F    C    |D           ||
In  the  state  I'm  in.
```

Verse 4

```
        G        D |F    G       |
How could  she  say  to  me
C                  |F    C      |
"Love  will  find  a  way?"
G    D      |F      G        |
Gather  'round,  all  you  clowns,
C                  |F    C    |D          |            ||
Let  me  hear  you  say:
```

Repeat Chorus

Outro
```
        G    D    |F    G    |C          |F     C      |

        G    D    |F    G    |C          |F     C    |G        ||
```

You and Your Heart

Words and Music by
Jack Johnson

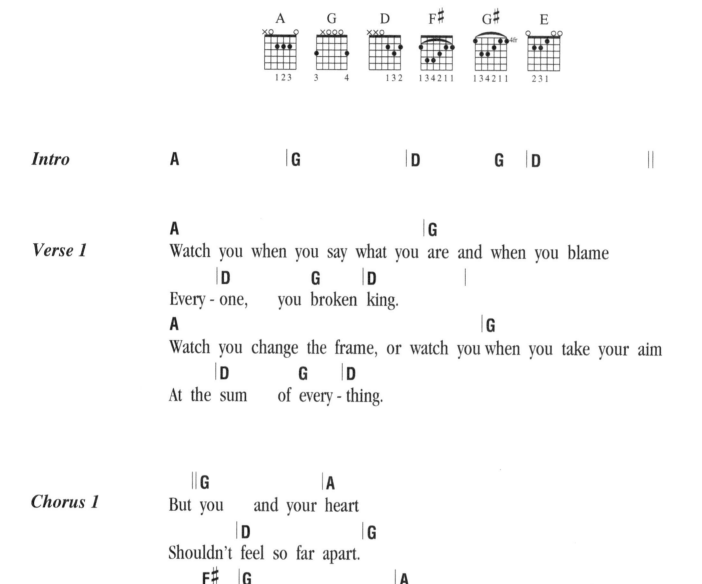

Intro   A |G |D   G |D ||

Verse 1

A |G
Watch you when you say what you are and when you blame
   |D   G |D |
Every - one,   you broken king.
A |G
Watch you change the frame, or watch you when you take your aim
   |D   G |D
At the sum   of every - thing.

Chorus 1

   ||G |A
But you   and your heart
   |D |G
Shouldn't feel so far apart.
  F# |G |A
You can't choose   what you take.
         |D |G G# ||
Why you gotta break and make it feel so hard?

Interlude 1   A |G |D   G |D |

                 A |G |D   G |D ||

Verse 2

```
        A                                 |G
Lay there in the street like broken glass reflecting pieces
         |D              G      |D
Of the sun;     you're not the flame.
                |A                        |G
You cut the people passing by because you know what you don't like.
         |D            G     |D
It's just so    easy.    It's just so    easy.
```

Chorus 2

```
        ||G            |A
But you     and your heart
            |D              |G
Shouldn't feel so far apart.
      F#  |G              |A
You can't choose    what you take.
               |D                      |G
Why you gotta break and make it feel so hard?
```

Chorus 3

```
        F# ||G                |A
Oh, and you     and your heart
            |D              |G
Shouldn't feel so far apart.
      F#  |G                |A
You can't choose    what you take.
               |D                  |G      G#      ||
Why you gotta break and make it feel so hard?
```

Interlude 2

```
    A    D     |A    D      |A    D     |A    D        |

    E             |
```

Outro

```
             ‖A              D
You draw so  many lines in   the sand,
         |A          D
Lost the fingernails on   your hands.
         |A              D
How you gonna scratch an - y backs?
        |A                  D              |E
Better hope the tide will  take our lines a - way.
        |E                |
Take all    our lines and…
A       D      |A     D              |
Hope the  tide will take our  lines a-…
A       D      |A     D        |E
Hope the  tide will take our  lines a - way.
        |E               |A          ‖
Take all    our lines away.
```